THE CHURCH SECRETARY:
Her Calling and Her Work

THE
CHURCH SECRETARY

Her Calling and Her Work

Katie Lea Myers

THE SEABURY PRESS · NEW YORK

To my husband and children,
who support me at all times and in
all things, and without whose love and
patience this book would not have been
possible.

PREFACE

The purpose of this book is twofold: To try to spell out for the church secretary the privileges given and the problems involved in commitment to the job of being part of that living organism which is the Church; and to help clergy and laity alike realize what it means for the secretary to give over and above that which is usually required in a similar, but secular, position. Necessarily, there will be practical helps to assist the church secretary in getting routine chores done in a systematic manner. Above all, I hope it will help her to determine her place in the mission of the Church. There are many ministries, and hers is one of them.

K.L.M.

CONTENTS

PART I:
The Church Secretary's Calling

Chapter 1

HER VOCATION AND COMMITMENT

> *It is well for a man to respect his own vocation whatever it is, and to think himself bound to uphold it, and to claim for it the respect it deserves.*
>
> CHARLES DICKENS

Not too long ago, the church or parish secretary was hired for almost any reason other than that she possessed the acumen to hold a position requiring business skill, patience, and love. In many instances, the minister or rector ended up with a lovable, aging spinster or widow who wanted to do something to fill her time, or with a part-time younger woman who needed experience. In either case, these secretaries generally proved themselves to be devoted and conscientious. Usually they were grossly underpaid because the board or vestry seriously wondered if the minister really needed help. I would be the first to offer tribute to those many women who gave hours "for Christ's sake" to churches which, even then, needed full-time assistance or a person with real executive ability.

In my own time, I recall few young women who

would consider a secretarial position in a church unless they had been unduly pressured by family or the
congregation. The position of church secretary was
reserved for the kindly, the considerate, the religious
—the woman who had reached that time in life
when she "knew" that she wanted to "serve." Once
they had chosen the secretarial or office profession,
most girls looked forward to insurance, law, or advertising. There they were more likely to find the
recognition not then accorded in the church. The
church was the place where one worshiped on Sun-
days, where youth meetings and the like were held;
but seldom did a young woman consider the frequently funereal atmosphere of the church office a
likely place to use her talents.

THE CHALLENGE OF HER VOCATION

Happily, all this is changing. More and more girls
and women who feel that they can use their business
skills to the glory of God are finding the position of
church secretary a rewarding one. They are not content to acquire only the regular office skills, but are
preparing themselves with a sound theological ap-
proach. One reason for the change is that more
women are looking realistically for the place where
they can make a contribution as committed persons
in the Church. For one to take a position as church

secretary without this feeling of commitment is only asking for frustration and irritation. To do this job well is most exacting. Where else can one find so many frequently conflicting personalities as are brought together daily in a church office? Business has them, but in business the designation of duties, salary scales, and the limitation of an eight-hour day are clearly defined.

In secretarial work—whether in a church or in business—personal traits and skills of a high order are required. No pastor, board, or vestry should consider a woman who apparently does not have understanding, self-control, patience, and sympathy. In fact, the woman contemplating a job in a church office as a vocation should very seriously ask herself some of these questions:

Am I sympathetic? Genuinely so?
Do I make quick judgments?
Am I too quick to form an opinion?
Do I show it when I am angry?
Am I impatient with others and their methods?
Am I a good listener?
Am I dependable?
Can I work under pressure?
Can I meet changes within the parish life with a quiet mind?
Do I brood if others do not follow my advice?
Can I accept criticism gracefully?

It is advantageous if the church secretary is a member of the same communion as that of the church where she works. In my opinion this is not an absolute requisite, but it helps in that she is, or should be, more familiar with her own denomination. However, I have known church offices managed by women of other faiths, and they often showed an objectivity that proved to be an asset. *The main thing is that the person on the job have the capacity to love.* This is more than simply being kind or having an "I like people" attitude.

When the church secretary becomes concerned with the *ultimate concern,* then her effectiveness begins. However perfect her work may be, however helpful, kind, and efficient she is, all this is simply preparatory to her meeting the world, where the meaning of her work and her understanding of right relationships are tested. Only there will she be able to *see* the unloved, the poor, the deprived. And there is a difference in seeing and *seeing*. One perhaps can see the big, sad eyes of a hungry child, but can one *see* the longing for love and help as well as for food? Can one *see* the pain and anguish of a man who is tormented, knowing that his child's life will be handicapped because his skin is not white? People with great burdens crowd in upon us, holding out their hands; but as my husband once put it, "The horrible possibility is that Christians will look directly at those eloquent hands and not see them."

The secretary must *see*, and this necessity applies whether her parish is in the city or the village, whether it is struggling to survive financially or endowed to the hilt.

THE CHURCH OFFICE—NOT A PLACE OF WITHDRAWAL

Seeing in this way will not be easy for the church secretary, just because of the very place where she works. Religious surroundings can in themselves be a deterrent to this. In his book *Honest to God,* John A. T. Robinson tells of his experience at a theological college. He had thought it would be easy there to spend time in prayer and meditation, to be away from the distractions of the outside world. And yet he found that seminary is one of the hardest places he had ever known in which to pray. He writes:

"For I discovered there what I can only describe as a freemasonry of silent, profoundly discouraged, under-ground opposition, which felt that all that was said and written about prayer was doubtless unexceptionable but simply did not speak to 'our' condition."

The secretary may find the church office to be just such a place, for often it is the very closeness of something that makes the doing harder. To join a protest against racial injustice may be easier than to invite a Negro neighbor in one's apartment building for a meal. One may tend a friend's child for a day and not see the loneliness in the eyes of one's own child. One may give hours to the sale of Easter seals and not a thought to the crippled newsboy at the door. The real danger, then, is being so caught up in our daily round that we miss the opportunity for this special kind of Christian action, "the sharing in the spirit" of the burden our *neighbor* bears.

THE CHURCH OFFICE—A PLACE OF ACCEPTANCE

I once knew a church secretary who had, it seemed, every secretarial qualification. Her ability to organize her work, to delegate duties, to compile reports, was enviable. She gave every evidence of listening and cooperation. She could not, however, accept people as they are. She could not accept the fact people would not or could not react as she thought they should. She could not accept the clergyman who made mistakes; she could not understand the parishioner who was unable to handle a family problem; she could not accept the fact that people were human beings, not things. I agree that the "persons and things" phrase has long been labored, but it is a worthwhile phrase for the parish secretary to bear in mind. Just recently, when I remarked that I loved something, my seven-year-old daughter said to me, "Mother, you like things and love people." I pray she will remember that truth past these tender years.

The secretary must accept people as they are, hard though she may find doing this. The office must be a place of acceptance, and the people who come there must know it. When acceptance is not genuine, people quickly recognize it as hollow and artificial. There is a difference between actually accepting or relating to another person and having a *feeling* that one does. One of the nicest compliments I ever received was paid me by a disturbed person to whom I talked and served coffee while he waited for his appointment. When, on leaving, he thanked me for the coffee and the pleasant wait, I knew that he was referring to more than that.

We all say quite glibly that we can identify with another person, put ourselves in his place so completely that we can see his problems; but *actual, realistic* identification is almost impossible. Can a person of middle-class background, adequate education, normal upbringing really identify with the slum dweller? He may live among slum dwellers, eat the same type of food, work in the same factory, but he knows that he can escape; he knows he can return to another way of life. The slum dweller knows that for him there is no other way of life. In such a situation complete identification is impossible, but there can be acceptance. One can accept another as his brother; one can grant him the dignity he deserves as a fellow man and a child of God; and if the acceptance is genuine, the other will know it.

Acceptance by the church secretary will bring with it some wonderful, some strange, some hilarious experiences. There will be things she knows she never will be able to change. There will be problems, many of which she will be able to solve and others that will trouble her conscience because she does not know what she should do. The people she serves, whoever they are, are the people "out there" in all walks of life with all the problems known to mankind.

THE INDISPENSABLES: LOYALTY, DISCRETION, AND HONESTY

In any parish there will at times be situations that the church secretary will have to accept nonjudgmentally; at other times there will be occasion for decisions made out of Christian conviction. At all times the church secretary must be a person of loyalty, discretion, and honesty. Why these qualities are so important we shall now consider.

First of all, the secretary knows the minister she works for probably better than anyone else, except his wife and family. She knows him as a man on the job, with all the frustrations of routines and schedules. She knows his anxieties and his love for his people. She knows his shortcomings as well as his best qualities. She knows when he is tired, happy, despondent, or bored. She knows him as a man, but she also knows him as her Father in God. Whatever kind of person he may be, as man or clergyman, he still is her Father in God, and she must be loyal to him.

The secretary knows the congregation, and the congregation should know her, and generally does. To her ears will come all those things that people want to convey indirectly to the minister. There has not been, nor will there ever be, a minister who is all things to all men. Some of his flock will want a mixer and caller; others, a man who calls only when he is requested to do so. Some will want an activist involved in community affairs; others, a pastor who works primarily with his own people. Some will want a gifted preacher; others, a man to whom they can talk. Inevitably suggestions and criticisms will be directed to the minister through the secretary. Her loyalty must be such that it can withstand any kind of attack or flattery. Some criticisms will be relevant, some not. What should she do? Should she keep all these things to herself? Or should she pass some on? This she must decide only after prayerful deliberation as to what will be constructive, and how the suggestion or criticism will affect and help the pastor. In such cases she must be wise and thoughtful lest she herself be judgmental or a bearer of tales.

I once knew a clergyman who apparently had not

accepted the responsibilities expected of a man who had taken the vows of ordination. Unknown to members of his congregation, he became involved in one questionable affair after another. He felt no compunction in calling the church office to cancel a daily service several hours before it was scheduled, simply asking that the secretary notify the usual "faithful." He would make a promise to a member of the congregation, and then tell his secretary he had no intention of keeping it. He was amused at how much he was able to get away with. This may not be an isolated case, for there are good and bad men in all professions. But such cases present a dilemma for the secretary. Does she reveal the clergyman's failings to an unsuspecting elder or warden? Does she seek other employment? Does she decide to stay on, trying to understand the motives behind the man's behavior, trying to help by example and gentle admonition, believing that this is where she belongs and that perhaps God has some plan for her at this particular time and place? Whatever her decision, when this man is in the sanctuary, regardless of the effort it may take on her part, he is God's representative, and this she must not forget. She must put out of her mind all thought of his personal inconsistencies and failures. She is not the judge. Naturally, she will not be able to dispel every thought every minute, any more than during a service one can put from one's mind the fleeting thought of how the Sunday roast is doing or gentle amusement at the contented look on the face of the old man snoozing during the sermon. But she must try.

Here are only a few examples of the kinds of situations that confront a church secretary. How can she help these people? How does she respond to them as a Christian?

Mrs. J. was one of the leading society women in the parish and community. She served, usually as a nonworking chairman, on many committees. She was known to make generous donations to many charities. She often invited the rector and vestrymen for elaborate and expensive dinners. She contributed many not-too-worn clothes to rummage sales. She served on the Stewardship Committee and worked to persuade others to pledge sacrificially to the Every Member Canvass. Yet the secretary knew that Mrs. J.'s pledge was a pitiable sum, and that at the end of the year it often went unpaid. Is the secretary's attitude toward Mrs. J. to be judgmental?

In one church office there worked a young man who was well liked, kind, good to the many children who came and went. He was not adquately prepared for a high position in the business world, but he did know his job in the church office. He labored overtime when necessary; he attended the services fairly frequently; he loved what he was doing and did it well. For many reasons he got into debt. Soon he was altering the books and mismanaging the accounts for which he was responsible. Parishioners knew the young man only as an upright, likable, supposedly honest person. He is under the supervision of the secretary, and she discovers what is happening. Does she advise his dismissal, leaving his friends in the congregation mystified and plunging him further into debt? Does she try to realize that the young man may be caught in overwhelmingly burdensome problems, that he is emotionally sick and is trying to extricate himself in the only way he sees open? How does she help him realistically?

The curate, a personable man, had made his place within the parish. A devoted minister, he performed his duties efficiently and with concern, ministering faithfully to the sick and shut-ins. He liked the particular parish where he served; he was also respected by the citizenry and worked hard for the betterment of the community. Now he has reached middle age, and there is not much chance that he would advance beyond the responsibility of curate. A young woman in the parish, burdened with guilt and afraid to talk to the rector lest she jeopardize the curate's future, admitted to the secretary that she loved the curate and that they had been intimate for a long time. What does the secretary advise the young woman to do? And what is the secretary's attitude now to be toward the curate?

A member of another congregation was a man in his late fifties. In his earlier years his personality and generous manner had won him many friends and acquaintances. A ready spender who enjoyed entertaining people, he had thrived on parties and counted a wide circle of friends. Suddenly his job lost its flavor. His lack of imagination and diversified interests made it probable that he would remain until retirement without further promotion. A real change then took place. He would break engagements repeatedly. He would make appointments and then ignore them. He began to find fault first with one acquaintance, then another, when the truth was that he was the offender. The number of his friends began to dwindle. He found himself growing older, becoming more lonely, unable to make new friends readily, and unwilling to become reconciled with the old ones. Soon he takes to spending much of his spare time in the church secretary's office, not acknowledging his loneliness and fears, but regaling her with tales of those friends whom he claimed either had wronged or deserted him. The secretary knows he will never see himself as he actually is. Does she just listen? Or fed up, does she tell him his own faults, thereby further isolating him? Or does she recognize a man probably spoiled in childhood, a victim of a broken home perhaps, whose actions and decisions may have been maneuvered for years by his aging mother?

Another parish had a choirmaster who had been employed on the recommendation of the minister.

He was an attractive young man, diligent in his work, above reproach in his conduct, a committed Christian in every respect. One day the minister approached him with an indecent proposal. In indignation, fury, and fear, the choirmaster then revealed what had happened to the secretary. In a situation like that what can she do? What should she do? Would not the congregation accept the minister's word against the choirmaster's? Should she get involved in such a touchy situation? Does her attitude to her employer change? Can she try to become a reconciler?

Then there was the case of a young girl whose father was a member of the vestry. He was a "pressure man," an executive in the advertising world. Her mother's time was filled with social engagements; her picture appeared often in the society sections of the local newspapers. Both parents had seen to it that their daughter had fine clothes and was taught the social graces. The girl was shy and retiring, more given to books than to dancing. Had it not been for the prestige of her family, no one would have given her a passing glance. At school she met a young boy who was unlike herself in that he was from a poor and humble background, but very much like her in his quiet and introverted ways. They worked together on a science project, and their acquaintance blossomed into a lovely and promising relationship. But with no love or understanding at home, the friendship turned into a burning adolescent love, and the girl became pregnant. Frightened of her father's reaction and her mother's wrathful scorn, she turned for help to the church secretary who had once been her Sunday-school teacher. Confused and desperate, she confided the news of her pregnancy. What is the secretary to do? She knows the rigid discipline imposed by the girl's parents. She knows the humiliation they will feel as a result of what they will consider "this disgrace." Does she avoid getting involved by suggesting that the girl see a social worker? Does she ask the girl to come to see her again when she is calmer so that the secretary will have time to think over the problem? Can she in any way help soften the wound for the girl and her parents? Should she go to the pastor? Through him can she be an instrument of reconciliation for this victim of the shortcomings of her parents?

Any church secretary will have similar experiences, some more dramatic, some less. But whatever the situation, she must be able to accept the person where he *is* and not demand that he be the kind of person she thinks he should be. Only then will her response be true acceptance. And whatever the situation, if she will let Him, God can and will work through her.

TESTED DAILY

As these few examples have made clear, the
church secretary is often in a position where she
deals more intimately with people than she would be
called upon to do in a regular business office. Daily
her decisions and actions will affirm or deny her
faith; daily what she says and does will reflect her
own personal life. Not only must her faith in God be
strong, but she must strive constantly to deepen it.
"He that cometh to God must believe that he is, and
that he is a rewarder of them that diligently seek
him." (Heb. 11:6) This will demand more of her
than merely being "religious."

Some church offices are distinguished by their
religious atmosphere—subdued conversation, frequent pious references, and an emphasis on devotion.
But are these offices really Christian? We all know
people who attend every church service unless they
are ill; read all the books recommended by the
clergy; live what neighbors consider a "good" life;
yet, despite all this, they are not truly Christian.
Why? Because they fail to relate what they do to life
itself. They pray, not pray with; they go to church
"to get something out of it," not to carry the Gospel
to the man on the street; they do good, not because
they *love* people, but merely to be neighborly. In

Light the Dark Streets, the question is asked, "Do we love them all, *all*—the hated and the haters, all victims, the disabled and the crippled? These are questions hard to ask and even harder to answer. . . . We must look, and although tears film our eyes, we must be strong and know what we are doing." Indeed, sometimes the church secretary may find herself being judged as "irreligious" because she has dared to make a decision prompted by her commitment to Christ and her understanding of God's will.

The difference between being religious and being a Christian is discussed by Bishop Robinson in *Honest to God:*

"Perhaps the best way to define 'religious' would be to ask, for instance, what is the difference between a religious film and a Christian film. Most people would without thinking tend to equate the two. But clearly there is an important distinction to be made. A Christian film is one that embodies Christian judgments on situations, Christian valuations of personal relationships, Christian insights into the purpose and meaning of life. A religious film is one that is about a certain area of experience or activity. It could have a biblical or quasi-biblical subject, it could be about nuns, or Lourdes, or center round some religious movement of experience. It is possible for the former category to have nothing specifically to do with religion at all, while the latter, as we know, can be nauseatingly and profoundly unchristian."

Much time can be spent in churchgoing, in prayer, and in attending religious functions, but the test of these actions is what they make one do and feel for his neighbors. The test of worship starts after the churchgoing, and its effectiveness is reflected in one's sensitivity to the Christ-less one, the lonely, the neglected. If worship has been something more than the achievement of a quiet, relaxed mood, then one can *recognize* the Christ-less, the lonely, the neglected. One's sensitivity has been prodded into a real awareness that there is more to life than "dressed-up religion." Instead of leaving the church with an inner sense of well-being, there will be in addition a creative urge to carry Christ beyond. God's purpose and His love for man will take on a new meaning. Then the act of worship will be turned outward to the relevance of Christian living. Religion will have become Christian commitment.

It is true that we consider worship and prayer essential; through them we increase our faith. I have said that the church secretary should be diligent in both, but she cannot stop there. The church building may be superb architecturally, the hymns beautiful, the sermons excellent, but unless all these are related to intelligent, loving concern outside the church walls, then the service ceases to be "holy." The worshiper, the secretary, must carry the love of Christ into the "secular" world. For the Christian the "holy" is the world itself, created holy by God Himself; and, through the power He has given to every man, His people must be loving, believing, responding, and reconciling people. Worship and prayer should reveal the real purpose of one's life, and help one realize it.

One does not worship in order to retire from the secular into the religious. And unless the church secretary—or any other Chrisitan—takes her place as a Christian in the world, she can do little to forward the very goal to which she has committed herself—namely, the spread of His kingdom. To the man in the street who does not know God's love, the church is withdrawn from the world—ineffectual. He will not be impressed by the "religious" Christian who defends this withdrawal. He looks to see Christ emerge not from Bible passages or church "handouts," but in the actions taken by church people who have been emboldened by their worship. "The man in the street," writes J. B. Phillips in *Your God Is Too Small,*

"thinks rather angrily along these lines: 'If there's a God at all, then He's here in the home and in the street, here in the pub and in the workshop. And if it's true that He's interested in me and wants me to love and serve Him, then He's available for me and every Tom, Dick, or Harry, who wants Him, without any interference from the professionals. If God is God, He's *big*, and generous and magnificent, and I can't see that anybody can say they've made a "corner" in God, or shut Him up in their particular box.'"

THE CHURCH SECRETARY'S COMMITMENT

The church secretary, then, must have the firm belief that every person is of equal worth in the eyes of God, and that every person, whether rich or poor, literate or illiterate, whole or torn apart, has the right to be treated with the respect and dignity due a child of God. This conviction demands more of one than pleasant office manners and decorum. It must rise out of prayerful dedication to Christ and His purpose. It can be acquired, I believe, only through personal commitment and devotional life. How can one be concerned genuinely with the burdens of others if she has not learned to face her own through prayer and meditation? Anyone knows that dealing with people and their problems is emotionally exhausting, and this is particularly true in church work, which is centered in people. The secretary who is refreshed for the day's task must first be refreshed spiritually. She should daily deepen her own spiritual life through reading the Scriptures and prayer, through the Church's Morning and Evening Prayer; she should attend divine services regularly; she should sustain herself through quiet days and meditation; she should be militant with other militants on issues related to the Church's mission. About her personal participation in parish organizations, I shall speak later.

The word *commitment* is often bandied about rather loosely. Many sermons have been preached about what commitment means. The advertising world nags the public about it through the printed word and through radio and television. PTAs, charities, friends, businesses, churches, all ask that we commit ourselves, our time, our money. Our lives are made up of one commitment after another. We commit ourselves to our husbands because we love them and because our union has been blessed in the sacrament of marriage. We commit ourselves to the well-being, education, and happiness of our children when we accept the responsibility of parenthood. We commit ourselves to the demands of friendship because we value companionship and trust. We commit ourselves to a profession or job because we need to earn money and wish to be useful and active. But none of these is the *real* commitment, which is the commitment to our Lord Jesus Christ. The intensity and depth of that commitment depends on the *measure* in which the person gives himself to Christ.

I once knew an old, partially crippled Negro woman who was so committed to her Christ that she felt the need to participate daily in the Holy Communion. Walking from her tenement when the weather was not too severe, spending carfare out of her meager old-age-pension allowance when she could not walk—rain or sunshine, biting cold or steaming heat, she was at His Table each morning. She *committed* herself—not her money, she had not enough sometimes for food; not her influence, she was only one of the thousands of poor on that city block. And one could see the result of this commitment in her lovely, serene, wrinkled, old face. She loved Christ and she was His. And she knew it and rejoiced in it despite poverty, despite pain, despite the drudgery and monotony of her lonely existence.

Commitment to Christ does not come easily. First, there must be the sincere yearning for Him. In his book *God in Us,* Miles Lowell Yates writes:

"It is, first, the *wanting,* and then, the *willing,* to do something more with one's life than just being alive and performing the inescapable duties or letting things take their course in and around us. It is having both the desire and the resolution to honor God with one's life. And dedication, of course, is an empty, a self-contradictory purpose, if it does not issue in activity, in all-around enterprise. Spiritual enterprise involves the whole man—the thinking, feeling, choosing, speaking, acting man. In a curious way, we have to enter *all* the events, if we are going to enter at all, even though we discover that we are better in meeting some challenges than others."

The church secretary must feel the need for this kind of commitment and be ready to seek to achieve it through self-examination and diligent searching.

One cannot tell another person how to proceed. It is a personal search, a personal inquiry, an opening of the mind and heart. The heart must be ready. "O God, my heart is ready, my heart is ready," cried the Psalmist (Ps. 108:1). So one must try to close one's eyes to everything outside and attempt to look at one's own self, without excuse, evasion, or rationalization. This is *me*. This is what I have done, and this is what I have not done. Slowly, deliberately, quietly, one looks at oneself and speaks privately to God. And one begins to know oneself in both despair and hope—despair for what one knows oneself to be, and hope for what one may become. And then the light will come, and He will be there, as surely as He came to St. John of the Cross:

> In this blissful night
> Secretly, no man seeing me,
> I see nothing,
> With no other light or guide
> But that which burned in my heart.
> And it led me
> Surer than the light of noonday.

Strengthened, then, by the emptying of oneself, slowly the conversation with Him can come. For many of us this is a slow and often painful thing. So it was also for many of the saints—a long, tortured path to the ecstasy of seeing Him.

We should perhaps recall here the profound insight which Evelyn Underhill makes in her meditations on the Lord's Prayer:

"God gives Himself mainly along two channels: through the soul's daily life and circumstances and through its prayer. In both that the soul must always be ready for Him; wide open to receive Him, and willing to accept and absorb without fastidiousness that which is given, however distasteful and unsuitable it may seem. For the Food of Eternal Life is mostly plain bread; and although it has indeed all sweetness and savor for those who accept it with meekness and love, there is nothing in it to attract a more fanciful religious taste. All life's vicissitudes, each grief, trial, and sacrifice, each painful step in self-knowledge, every opportunity of love or renunciation and every humiliating fall, have their place here. All give, in their various ways and disguises, the heavenly Food. A sturdy realism is the mark of this divine self-imparting, and the enabling grace of those who receive."

When true commitment is present, there is also present the desire to worship God in His community; there is a direct correlation between commitment to Jesus Christ and worship in His Church. For such worship is not our (or my) worship, it is the Church's worship, the worship and prayer of the Body which is Christ, to the Father. To participate in that worship is truly to know His presence, which is refreshment indeed. No commitment can survive without this sustenance.

Strengthened through her own devotional life, the parish secretary will find she can humbly offer her abilities to God for His use. For she has a vocation *and* a commitment. Daily she will raise her life to the level of God, which is the way of seeing how each of the multitude of small choices becomes a part of her response to God's call. It is this offering of the whole of her life which will break down barriers between herself and others. "Saints are people," one theologian tells us, "who find holiness in the tiniest matters —who take every choice seriously because it is part of their life-long dialogue with God."

Chapter 2

HER MINISTRY

> *He who has God*
> *Finds he lacks nothing:*
> *God alone suffices.*

A job is a job is a job is a job. Most people try to find the type of job that will be most creative and fulfilling for them. Most people try to give an honest day's work for the wages received. But the job is only a job to the person who does not and cannot see beyond the day's labor a working out of God's purpose for the individual. Bishop James A. Pike has aptly expressed this in *Liturgy Is Mission:*

"Personal fulfillment, yes: I have a job and I am glad that I have a job that I enjoy. And that is fine—there is nothing wrong with that. But when we look at it from the biblical perspective, that same work can have a much more profound meaning in terms of God's eternal purpose that the Creation be finished, that all men be redeemed and healed, and that all men be in community. . . . Therefore, each of these acts of work . . . is part of the eternal purpose rather than merely part of the passing show."

Work can be just work, efficiently carried out, boring, personally rewarding, exhausting, or fulfilling. It can call for the backbreaking output of strength or the skilled knowledge of the professionally trained. Whatever the work, it can, and should be, a *ministry.*

THE MEANING OF MINISTRY

Until recent years, *ministry* was thought of only in terms of the clergy. Perhaps they were content to have it so, either out of fear of jeopardizing their own position and influence or because they did not know just what to do about it. But today the picture is changing. More and more lay people are waking up to the fact that one does not have to be ordained to *minister.* More and more lay people are committing themselves to offer to God their lives, home, work, talents in the realization they are called of God to do so. The lay person's role in ministry is now recognized as a duty. The ministry of the laity could be the sleeping giant that will help transform the function of the Church, because, as we are beginning to rediscover, it is an essential part of the function of the Church.

In the Early Church the faithful were lay people. Some had great gifts; all had varied talents. Some were strong, some weak. But they were ministers to others and sharers of the Gospel according to their individual ability. They were "called" and they answered, but there is no indication that some did not continue in, or later return to, their "secular" lives. The significance of this is clear, for it is the lay person in his daily life and work who meets people, and when in this meeting he bears Christian witness among those who are not churchgoing, he is not merely a church member but an effective missioner of the Church.

To minister is to serve, simply that: to serve other men in all walks of life, within the Church and without. Ministry becomes relevant only when the layman sees ministry from the servant's standpoint. William Stringfellow puts it this way: "The real issues of faith have to do with the everyday needs of men in the world and with the care for service of those needs, whatever they may be, for which the Church exists."

WOMEN IN THE CHURCH

The extent to which the church secretary's role and ministry are recognized may depend a great deal upon how the members of the parish regard the role and ministry of women generally in the Church. In some denominations and some parishes this recognition is graciously accorded. In many others, however, there still lingers the tendency to think of women in quite unchristian terms, as an inferior class of being capable only of minor functions.

Too many parishes continue to see women members as capable only of raising money, working as teachers, caring for altars and sanctuaries, making and maintaining choir vestments, or performing other time-consuming duties suitable to the female sex and not worthy of the time and attention of the men of the congregation. Many clergymen have become accustomed to depend solely on women for almost all of the jobs in the church needed to be done except for those requiring decision-making such as serving on a board or vestry. The men of the parish will consider it their duty to attend services with some degree of regularity, to be present at the annual meeting, to contribute to the budget, to serve a term on the governing board of the congregation. They are inclined to leave the countless other duties —the dinners, the bazaars, the collection of food for the needy, the baby tending, the pageants, the rummage sales—to their wives and other women.

Today, however, many women are beginning to ask whether the time and energy expended on these projects and in attending an endless series of study sessions, devotional readings, bandage rollings, and Lenten programs truly contribute to the *mission* of the Church or to *meaningful* worship.

In fact, intelligent and capable women are beginning to tire of the superficiality of much of women's work in the church. Like many young people who wander away from youth groups because the pro-

grams are so undynamic, women are becoming tired
of the unchallenging, boring, and basically unimportant role that has been allotted them. After making
important contributions in government and in the
business world, where they have been allowed to become really involved, the ineffectual lot left to them
in church affairs grows impalatable and certainly
unchallenging to many.

According to Carol Kleiman's study, published in
the October, 1964, issue of *Renewal:*

"There are vast numbers of women who are disenchanted
with the Church, who view its activities as inconsequen-
tial and historically unimportant. If such a realization is
painful, it may help churches to learn that people reject
the Church not because it is too involved in human problems, but because it is not involved enough. For every
woman who feels 'at home' with present structures, there
is one who does not, who looks elsewhere for a chance to
fulfill herself and her mission in the world."

Let it also be noted that large groups of women
are today in no way attached to the church. In the
same issue of *Renewal*, Peggy Way points out the
significance of how many *types* of women are now
conspicuously missing from the church:

"The single women in large numbers; working women,
single and married; the younger college graduate groups;
mothers whose children attend the church Sunday
Schools but who do not have the appropriate clothing nor

feel within the 'circle'; Negroes and members of other minority newcomer groups frequently living closer to the church geographically than the older members, but 'assumed to want to be with' their own kind."

It may truly be said that women are looking for renewal of the church and new areas of involvement more urgently and more generally than are men. The growing prominence of women in political and business areas makes the lack of this prominence in the church's real life even more conspicuous. Women are struggling to understand the real purpose of their efforts. Peggy Way continues her argument:

"Is hemming diapers around the lunch table really attacking the social realities of our time? Does the old clothes-toys-food syndrome reflect sacrificial giving or the seeking after cheap grace, far removed from the human and social realities of the receivers? Can a racially segregated Church and community—whether in the suburbs or inner city—offer to Christian people the type of life experiences most crucial to them? Does the Church's involvement in the city and in contemporary culture recognize that this is God's gift and challenge and not God's curse?"

She concludes that the churches are not addressing themselves to the

"frightfully real questions that today's women—in and outside the Church—are asking. How can I raise my children to be healthy and socially conscious persons, with a strong enough sense of identity to withstand and counter the negative aspects of contemporary pressures? What is the meaningful life for the widow or the wife of the retired man, facing ten to twenty years of 'leisure time'? How does the single woman cope with her own sexuality in a world in the midst of a revolution in morals? How does one combine commitment to family with commitment to vocation—a tension brought about by the increased educational achievements of today's women? How can the housewife best stand with her husband, understanding his world and its fragmentation and helping him to keep whole even as she seeks for him to enter meaningfully into her more home-bound experiences? And how can a deeply personal religious faith be held in tension with profoundly significant action in the name and with the strength of that Faith?"

These are some of the questions being asked by women everywhere in our churches. When "renewal" and "involvement" are discussed, it is often the women who speak more relevantly and knowledgeably than their husbands. Certainly women have taken direct action by challenging the clergy for answers, by demanding more understanding and acceptance from laymen, by standing beside men on picket lines to highlight the Church's failure to combat racial injustice, political bigotry, poverty, and other burning issues of our day. Some men, even those who are ready to turn over the family budget and the rearing of children to women, are quite reluctant to listen when women speak up about what is needed in the churches of today. They cannot accept, it seems, the involvement of women in the worldly, everyday decisions and relationships which many women somehow see as part of their mission.

Peggy Way writes:

"The real question is whether church women are helped to go out into secular society, strengthened by those understandings of feminine (and Christian) identity, sexuality, commitment and personhood which are part of the Church's heritage—and whether they can carry the ministry of the Church beyond itself, into the world where it rightfully belongs."

It is the time *now* for churches to examine more fully the place of women in the Church. Many women are no longer going to be willing just to "join 'em." What energies they possess they are going to use in issues pertinent to the day. With the realization that their children must face the realities of life on a "gutsy" level, they are no longer content to be kept from experiencing these realities themselves. Voter registration, school standards, urban and suburban juvenile delinquency, criminal statistics, housing: these are the issues before men and before *women*, and women are ready to go out from the churches to confront these problems.

The churches, then, must be willing to re-evaluate the status of women. If they do so honestly, they may find themselves equipped with a powerful and dedicated lay ministry whose strength they have

long overlooked except for doing those nonessential
jobs without which the Church would still exist. And
among those so dedicated will be found the church
secretary.

THE OPPORTUNITIES TO SERVE

The church secretary is in a position to make a
contribution to the Church's ministry that can be
both meaningful and unique. Nowhere is there a
riper field for harvest than the parish office. There
will be opportunities for her to serve, to show her
strength, to express her concern, to use her imagination. Here many come for advice, comfort, information, help. Like Dorcas of Joppa, she can be "full of
good works"; and like Priscilla and Aquila, a "helper
in Christ Jesus." She is where the situations are!
They may be the pastor's ultimate responsibility, but
she, too, can meet real needs in the very way she
responds to the people who call on the telephone or
who come through the office door. If she is a sensi-
tive and committed person herself, she will be able
to offer reconciliation instead of judgment, to see the
heartaches, despairs, and hopes that so often are the
human lot.

A stranded, broken derelict of a man, in from the
street, seeks help in getting to his destination.

A frantic mother asks the church's help in finding her teen-age son, who has been missing three days.

The telephone rings to bring a father's halting announcement that his daughter has been killed in an automobile accident.

A church school teacher wants to discuss an imagined grievance against the director of religious education.

A young couple, new to the neighborhood and unchurched, stop in to inquire about marriage.

A child is injured while playing in the churchyard.

The sexton, harried with too many duties, seeks advice as to whom he should try to please—the pastor or "all those meddling women."

The town drunk drops in for the price of a cup of coffee.

The report comes that two boys have been drowned on a church-organized outing.

The organist stops by to unload some of his frustration about members of the congregation who do not like his music.

The mother of five visits the office to find out where she can get information on planned parenthood.

A policeman comes looking for data on the pilfered alms box.

A tearful choir boy, two dollars in hand, asks if it is enough for the weekend camping trip.

These are important issues to the people involved, and the secretary must see the need in each instance. The right word, the right decision, the right manner, the right concern, depend upon her.

The kind of problems people bring to a church office will vary depending on where the church is located. But *wherever* the office, people will come so long as it is a place of acceptance, and the role of the secretary is to make it one.

I once knew a secretary whose office skills were only average, but who made up for it in her ability to minister to people. One day she was confronted with a young woman, a well-known professional worker in the community, who arrived in hysterics, threatening to destroy herself and recognizably seriously ill. That secretary, unable to locate the pastor, literally talked the young woman into calmness. At times using actual physical restraint, at other times cajoling, quietly she talked and talked, hour after hour, holding the woman until the pastor arrived and the woman could be hospitalized.

I knew another secretary who, when asked by a waiting parishioner for a cup of coffee, remarked that she was not there to serve. Her idea of her position not only was exalted; she would let nothing interfere with her office procedures. There was no time in her day for people, only for routines. She could not visualize that the request for coffee may have been an attempt to open the door for a much-needed conversation, a cry for help, a confidence to be shared.

Another secretary who did her work very well was gracious and understanding and helpful—to adults. She had nothing against children as long as they did not bother or interrupt her. Her days went well until the released-time children arrived. Unknowingly and without malice, they made her office untidy, and then she would fly into a rage, berating them severely. She could not see that a pleasant reminder might in time have improved the situation, or that the children, if requested to do so, would have helped tidy up the place. She would not take the time to try. Her tempers continued, the released-time attendance diminished, and the many mothers to whom she was always gracious kept wondering why their youngsters disliked the church secretary so much.

Assuredly, the routine matters of the day must be taken care of. Every church secretary knows that she has the responsibility of seeing that certain things are accomplished each day. Letters, appointments, telephone calls, records—these are part and parcel of the business of any office, large or small. With most secretaries in the business world such responsibilities are absorbed as part of the normal routine. There are, of course, the usual interruptions: dictation is delayed, lunch hours are changed, rush reports must be completed. But for the parish secretary, as contrasted to the average business secretary, the unexpected is the rule rather than the exception, and she is always involved in trying to keep some semblance of a planned day. The reminders, ticklers, calendars, and follow-up files so familiar to the Girl Friday sometimes get thrown out the window as one crisis follows another. The crisis may not be as serious as the parish house catching on fire, but it may be as important as giving time to a teen-ager and his problem or receiving with dignity the skid-row character asking for money for food. To the teen-ager or the derelict it is a crisis. The secretary's ministry to those who come to the church office is as important, often more so, than all the other duties which, as an efficient secretary, *she must perform with dispatch.*

DAILY OCCASIONS OF MINISTRY

There will be many situations that on the surface do not appear to be important. Take the "bum" I mentioned. Wherever the church is located, there is always the man, down and out, who comes asking for help. Think what it must do to his pride to have to beg. Think of the degradation he undergoes on the streets from people who give no thought to why he is a derelict. And think what it must do for such a man to be treated for once with dignity. Who knows what society contributed to bring him to his low position?

Whatever conditions led him to his empty, aimless life, whether it was through his own fault or the faults of others, he is still a man, a person. As a human being—yes, made in the image of God—even he deserves not just kindness but dignity. The way in which the church secretary receives the derelict can either be just another blow to his seemingly hardened front or it can lift him again—if only for a few moments—to the place in which he is like other men. It is true that not all transients are trustworthy. I, and other secretaries probably, have had unfortunate experiences with some. However, these instances are not too frequent. Most down-and-outers are interested only in getting their hungry stomachs filled and gaining the necessary carfare to another community where they think there may be a better day.

The alcoholic is another frequent visitor to the church office. Sometimes it is because he thinks another talk with the pastor may help. Often it is because he needs money for another drink. There are alcoholics in every community and city. When yours comes to the church office, he probably has a splotched face, bleary eyes, several days' growth of beard, and trembling hands. Already he feels he can hardly make it. His stomach is in turmoil, his headache almost unbearable. He is sure a drink is just the thing he needs to feel better. Often he is not a pleasant sight, and it would be an easy thing to give him the price of a beer and send him on his way with hardly a greeting. But the alcoholic, too, is a person, and for that reason he should be treated with dignity.

When I was living in a vicarage on the Lower East Side of New York, there was an alcoholic who made the church his first place of visit in the morning after he left his flophouse bed. He came for money to buy his cup of coffee. Almost daily he attended the early service. He rang the church bell for the service, and his Amens were heard above all others—though Joe never made his communion. Wherever he may have wandered during the day, at mealtime he showed up at the vicarage. Joe knew what he was, but he wanted to be a person again. I conceived the idea of paying him a small fee to take the dog out for a walk each morning. It bothered me to see him have to ask for money each day, and this arrangement would spare him that humiliation. For a few weeks the system worked splendidly, until I found that Joe was not taking the dog for walks at all. He always wanted his coffee money first thing, and I assumed he got his coffee on the walks. Joe, however, was hastily putting the dog in a room in the parish house and proceeding to quench his thirst. When I felt it necessary to speak to him about his dishonesty, he became indignant and for weeks refused to speak to me. The outdated newspaper clippings and daily notes to me, poorly typed on some battered old machine, no longer appeared under my door. The truth is, Joe's being angry with me hurt me as much as it did him. Of course, I had to speak to him about his deception. Of course, he was an alcoholic; neither I nor anyone else could change that. But to me Joe was a person and deserved to be treated with the dignity due every man.

Another habitué of the parish office, and one to be seriously reckoned with, is the neurotic man or woman who, when emotionally beset, uses the church secretary as a whipping post. The kind of person I am talking about is usually able to hold a fairly responsible job and to cope with life socially, but when having a "spell," he or she becomes a serious and exhausting problem. Having spent his ire on his family or business associates—who have finally shut their ears to his laments and complaints— this type of person turns to the one place left where he feels he can pour out his wrath, the church office. This puts the secretary in a difficult and treacherous position. The majority of the time the man is a good citizen, dutiful in his parish responsibilities, mindful of his neighbor and those in need; but with uncanny regularity he seems to need to work out his hostilities in words if not in deeds.

When I was a parish secretary I knew one such woman. She was intelligent, well educated, well versed in community affairs, exceptionally helpful in parish organizations. She would continue for weeks on an even keel—jovial, friendly to everyone, helpful. Then would come the deluge! All people and things came under her condemnation. It was as though she was permeated with evil. She delighted, it seemed, in her anger and contempt. At times, when she was in this mood, her friends and the clergy were tempted to abandon her. She would spend hours in and around the church wreaking havoc with her accusations and innuendos. Relationships would be strained and feelings trampled. But Marge was a person! There were many personal problems that goaded her conscience. Although of a good background, she had of her own choice seen much of the seedy side of life in a misdirected attempt to know herself. She befriended many a person who needed food and housing, but she found it hard to accept real friendship. She doubted and was doubted. She reviled and was reviled. She cut off others and was herself cut off from human kindnesses. But, in spite of herself, Marge was accepted as a person at the church. She came to know this; she came to know herself, even though the moods continued. She could not control them, and most of the time she did not want to do so, but she knew that even at those times she was a person to the church as fully as when she presented her better self. The church secretary will encounter many Marges in one form or another, and she has a ministry to each of them.

There are many people, especially women, who

reach a point when they feel their usefulness has passed. Their children have grown up and moved away. Their husbands are caught up in trying to compete with younger men in business. One by one their contemporaries succumb to the afflictions of old age. Time is taking its toll, and time lies heavy on their hands. Often such women turn more and more to the church office, where there is activity, friendliness, acceptance. This is one of the most difficult types the church secretary has to deal with. There is nothing really wrong with a woman in this plight. She is in good health, but she is not happy, and she feels sorry for herself. She wants to get outside her empty home and be with someone who will listen. After all, she is going to the women's meeting at the church anyway, and a visit to the office is just the thing to lift her spirits. These visits may require long-suffering and patience on the secretary's part. She is already behind in typing the board minutes or mimeographing the bulletin. Mrs. D needs attention and reassurance, and however monotonous and tedious and boring she may be to the secretary, Mrs. D should get that attention and reassurance. While her need is not pressing or critical, it is real. Mrs. D needs to have an hour's visit where she knows that she is welcome and where she glimpses again her past years of usefulness. The parish secretary must be wary. It is often easy not to *see* the Mrs. D's.

There is little place for children in the ordinary

business office. True, the boss may bring his young son in on the way to a ball game. The young executive's wife may bring her children by for a moment "to see where Daddy works." The church office is another story. Children always find their way there from the parish house, particularly the loner, the mixed-up, the rejected. It can be tiresome at the end of a busy day to be left with a child who is waiting at the office for the return of his working mother, or a child reluctant to go back to a dreary home and a belligerent parent. When she is weary and frustrated by work still undone, the church secretary needs extra strength and untiring patience to give of herself to these children. John and Sue and Bill must have the time, the acceptance, the love that the "church house" can give them—through its secretary—even if it means the letters must be typed at home at night or the correspondence filed before office hours the next morning.

When the parish secretary opens her door each morning, she is "in action." Being in action means ministering. As I have said, ministry is a serious duty, for which all Christians have a responsibility. By virtue of her position the parish secretary has a decisive and important opportunity as well as responsibility. Seldom will there be a day that she will not be asked to face people in need—bitter people, grieving people, sick people, anxious people, sarcastic people, lonely people, poor people, rich people, inquiring people, lost people. She must, remembering the examples of Jesus and St. Paul, use what insight she may have to see their problems and to demonstrate God's love through love. "As every man hath received the gift, even so minister the same one to another, as good stewards of the manifold grace of God." (I Peter 4:10)

SPECIAL OCCASIONS: DEATH AND ILLNESS

Often the information about the death of a member of the congregation comes first to the church office. Death is always a trying time for the family of the deceased. Apart from the shocking realization of final physical separation, the very fear of death itself and the painful duty of making necessary preparations must be faced. Strangely, thousands of people go happily through life, without making any provisions for their own demise or for that of other members of their family. If the minister has not been present at the hospital or home when the death occurs, every effort must be made to notify him immediately so that he can be with the family. The secretary should tactfully advise the family to await his aid. Usually, most parish offices know—they definitely should know—undertaking establishments that are reliable and trustworthy. The secretary should ask if the parish office can make any sugges-

tions. This may save misunderstandings and prohibi-
tive expense. The parish secretary herself should
visit the bereaved family, offering her assistance.
Some secretaries think that after all details have
been handled, her role is over. Not so. As a member
of the Body of Christ, the Church, she must comfort
the grieved as St. Paul admonished the Thessalo-
nians: "Wherefore comfort one another."

It need not be emphasized that the church secretary should know what arrangements must be made
for burial services. As soon as the arrangements have
been completed, either through the minister or
through her, she can begin the routine of advising
the sexton, the organist, and any other people whose
services will be required. All information concerning
the deceased and the service should be readily available, so that telephone inquiries can be answered
promptly. Needless to say, the name of the deceased
should be removed immediately from the church
mailing list. It is distressing to a family to receive
mail addressed to the deceased, whether or not he or
she attended regularly.

Sickness, too, takes its toll, both of the patient and
of the anxious family. When any member of the congregation is injured or falls ill, the pastor and other
clergymen on the staff should be notified, and the
person's name placed on the prayer list. Particularly
can the secretary be of assistance if a family requests
help in gaining admittance to a hospital. The secre-

tary should know how to take care of this emergency. She should ascertain from the relatives whether the doctor has recommended, either in writing or through a call to the admissions office, the patient's admittance. If the patient is destitute, she should know if the parish is prepared to assume part of the cost of hospitalization. If the parish is not in a position to help, she should know on whom to call for welfare aid. Time can be important in such situations, and knowing what to do may save a life.

The secretary should have handy at all times a list of clinics, of visiting nurse and ambulance services. These telephone numbers should be displayed so that they can be found quickly should the secretary be absent from her desk. Knowing the name of a particular person to call in each of these categories can expedite the transaction.

Everyone knows that it is difficult to deal at length with persons who are chronically ill. It takes patience and resourcefulness to hear the constant complaints that are usually characteristic of the chronically sick. Many of these people are able to be up and about some of the time, and may seek solace at the church. Often they will visit the church office, hoping to see the minister. In his absence, they talk to the secretary, pouring out the long list of symptoms which they have related over and over on other occasions. It takes a sympathetic secretary to give her time and ear again and again to this kind of person.

RESPONDING TO THE ELDERLY AND THE ANXIOUS

Many elderly and anxious people come to the church. Where else can they go? Very often the elderly are alone; usually they are lonely. They need reassurance that they are not forgotten. I have seen them by the thousands on the subways and buses, with that resigned but desolate look on their faces. They are not like children, who are able to forget quickly. For the elderly, memories are often all they have left. The parish secretary should try to get them interested in a club or activities for older people. She could help pave the way for the timid by finding some member of the congregation to take them to the first meetings. She should have a list of homes for the aged, the names of practical nurses who work with older men and women, employment agencies that sometimes hire elders for part-time jobs, the names of volunteer groups who provide entertainment or recreation for groups of older people. When older people visit the office, she can be tender and loving, a willing listener to the oft-repeated tales of another day.

The anxious! Today, even people blessed with all the necessary comforts of life are anxious. But what of the poor, the dispossessed, the loner, the multiple-problem family, the unemployed, those with language handicaps in a new community? Here again the secretary needs an established relationship with social service agencies, institutions, family and child consultation centers; she needs the addresses of government offices. These are her tools, but they must be used *only* as tools. Her first concern must be the individual himself, his need for love as well as for physical help, his right to a place in the sun.

INVOLVEMENT IN CHURCH GROUPS

I spoke earlier about the personal involvement of the secretary in the affairs of the congregation. I have said that she should be active with others active in *movements* that grow out of the church's concern. There are those who think that because the secretary is on hand she should be active in all of the *organizations* of the congregation. This would be unwise, and also impossible. No one has that much time, nor is anyone physically able to attend all the meetings held in a parish. As a member of the congregation, the secretary is required to choose and to participate only in as many activities as any other parishioner might. How easy it is for a group to ask the parish secretary to take minutes or type reports. After all, she is there. Day by day the secretary will have the opportunity of meeting and working with presidents or chairmen of various lay groups, and she should have a general knowledge of what each group is doing. But she should function actively in these groups only if she herself chooses to do so, not because it is expected of her. There will, of course, be meetings and organizations which the minister leads. If he wants her to do so, she should attend, lending her help and interest. In such cases, the minutes and agendas and other necessary preparations fall within her province.

The secretary will have to use discretion in refusing certain requests. In some instances, it may be necessary for the minister to refuse on her behalf. If the parish is large and has many organizations, there will be requests from the women's groups, the laymen, the church school teachers, and others for typing and mimeographing. She will have to decide which of these she can handle in addition to her regular chores. A warning! Once the door to such requests is open, it is difficult to close it again. This is where the minister can draw the line, so the secretary does not fall heir to chores which should be done by the groups themselves. Without offending any one person or organization, he can announce that each group must be responsible for its own announcements, booklets, and correspondence. In many cases lay men and women have access to secretarial help, but even if they do not, they can delegate all but extraordinary chores to their own members. I am not saying that the secretary should not attempt to be as helpful as she can, nor am I saying that the activities of the organizations are not important. What I am saying, and I speak from experience, is that the secretary often is called upon and expected to do many tasks which, first of all, she does not have time to do, and, secondly, which are not her responsibility simply because she is the parish secretary. This is sometimes difficult for the average layman to understand, for often he does not realize how many things go on in the church office over and above getting out the bulletins and posting the pledge envelopes.

For instance, I think at once of the Altar Guild. The secretary should be allowed to choose if she wishes to participate in this honored and devoted work. I know secretaries who have been asked to join the Altar Guild just so they would be nearby in case the woman on duty could not make the necessary preparations. A member of the Altar Guild should no more call on the church secretary to substitute for her than some woman who lives a mile from the church. In these circumstances, the secretary becomes merely a handy substitute, rather than a full-fledged member of the Guild, and it will not take long for her attitude toward the Altar Guild and its members to change.

It may be hard to understand why one little request can seem burdensome. Add to it the many daily requests from others, however, and soon the secretary's work load is more than she can possibly handle. Not only does she become overtired and irritated, but the parishioners become frustrated and critical when the work is not completed on time.

CALLED BY GOD

The secretary, then, should regard her role as a ministering one. She is not merely a technical helper to the ordained clergyman. She has a dignity all her own in the Body of Christ. Indeed, the serious secretary in a parish is "called" to her work. She must have a sense of vocation if she is to be more than a technician. She must feel a part of the action—and never look upon her role as unimportant. Some may object that the use of the word *ministry* is incorrect in describing her role. It is true, the word is seldom used to describe *any* woman's work in the Body of Christ. But the Church is itself ministry. The Church is first and foremost a Servant Church in which all its members are ministers. And since women are "of the laity," as many writers have recently been reminding us, women, too, are numbered among the ministers in Christ's Church.

Perhaps if this were understood on all sides, life in the miniature Body, the parish, would be smoother. The secretary would be given her due dignity by those parishioners who tend to view her simply as the parish "work horse." She would not be a threat even to the most disorganized pastor. She would have a place respected by all.

But this ideal may not come to pass until we understand that all the baptized are commissioned as ministers. It was not only the Church of the Middle Ages that became dominated by the ordained clergy. The contemporary Church also is organized in such a way that most of the balls are thrown by the clergy and caught by the laity. The average clergyman's self-image is that of *the* parish leader, in all phases of parish life. And the laity by and large, as well as many members of the clergy, are content to have it so. But the Church is the *laos*, that is, People. Even archbishops belong to the *laos*, not to mention church secretaries. Their functions differ, to be sure, but each has his claim to ministry. The whole Body ministers in the unity which the Head of the Body provides.

The secretary who conceives of her role as one of ministry, who is willing to be a servant in the real sense, becomes a great influence in the community of the church. Her Christian witness becomes an example to others. She is the type of committed person that Layton Zimmer has described in *On the Battle Lines:*

"Such laymen invariably come to exercise great influence in the life of their parish, not through office or power but through witness and example. They soon begin to take an increasingly conscientious burden on themselves to reflect their convictions of Christ in their given vocation. In the deepest terms of ministry, these people become a pool of concern, response, and imaginative action —a real Faithful Remnant in the life of the Christian community."

PART II:
The Church Secretary's Work

Chapter 3
HER JOB AND
RELATIONSHIPS

> *When men are rightfully occupied, their amusement grows out of their work.*
>
> JOHN RUSKIN

In any office, the employer has the prerogative of determining what the responsibilities of his secretary shall be and how she shall perform certain tasks. Sometimes the employer and the secretary will differ in their views about how a task is to be done. But these differences of opinion when frankly discussed can be the way toward better mutual understanding. On the whole, though, employer and secretary should have a cooperative and agreeable relationship if the secretary's position is to be an honored and satisfying calling. The knowing and intelligent church secretary should be able to go far beyond the routine tasks which the minister has a right to expect, and wise and fortunate is the minister who allows her to do this and thereby to increase his own effectiveness. In order to allow it, however, he must be free from the fear that she will usurp his role. Most clergymen have not had business training. They go from seminary to a small parish or, in the

role of assistant, to a larger one. Sometimes the secretary strikes such a man as a threat, especially if she
is capable and experienced. Wise is the clergyman
who willingly works with his secretary to form an
effective and happy team.

UNDERSTANDING THE MINISTER'S VOCATION

Basic to doing well the job of church secretary is
to have an understanding of the ministerial vocation
—what it means to be a clergyman, and what
prompts a man to choose this demanding, sometimes
unrewarding, often physically and emotionally exhausting, profession. Except in the intimacy of his
own family or in the companionship of others in the
same profession, the minister generally is considered
to be a public person. Usually, he is a person who
has accepted the role of servanthood. This may be
hard for lay people to understand because the ministerial profession is generally accorded respect, defer-
ence, and social acceptance. But the minister himself
knows, or ought to know, what his role really is. The
minister who is true to his vocation will put his ministry above all other things. At times this can be a
terrific strain both on him and on his family, *but the
choice must be made*. Making the choice may sound
easy to the layman, but the clergyman who accepts

the vows of the servant ministry knows the many complexities he faces in trying to be true to his commitment. He is faced constantly with decisions and problems, not only about money and administration but, more important, about people. His life and thought are centered on his flock—his people. They become his, so to speak, and he should become theirs. They have the chief claim on his life and his time. When he is thus wrapped up in their lives, then the relationship of pastor and people is marked by deep and mutual understanding and trust.

The modern minister is quite different from the minister of a few decades ago. Then the parson was the man of God, the judge, the preacher. He visited the sick and shut-ins, comforted the mourning, spent much time in reading the Bible, in theological study, and in directing the affairs of his church and congregation. Sometimes he was so stern and intolerant of sin that one sought his counsel only with fear and trembling. His word was law in the church, and he spoke with authority to his people. The minister today does not attempt to fill his role in that way. He is still the man of God, only sometimes the judge, and often but not always the preacher. He takes care of the sick to be sure, and the mourners also. He acknowledges the presence of sin all about. But he is a modern man. He is aware of inadequacies in the school system; he knows which precinct officials are lax; he has suffered from the duplicity often practiced by the community's politicians. He is aware, too, that he is not perfect, that he sometimes fails to be as patient or wise or kind as he wants to be, and that he sometimes fails to lead his people in responsible public witness. He is involved in and concerned about community, national, and world affairs. He is many faceted—or so it is to be hoped—and his interests are as broad as the modern world.

The good secretary knows all sides of her employer and all aspects of his interest and concern. She knows that in addition to doing her office chores she is a part of his daily experience, and that she can therefore be either an asset or a hindrance to him. He needs her knowledge and her help. The wise church secretary also knows that she cannot discover her own vocation *out of relationship* to her pastor's calling.

A theological understanding of the Church, then, will help a church secretary understand the minister she works for. It will help her understand herself and her place in the Church. When she knows that the Church is *first*, that the congregation is the miniature Body of Christ, that the Church is not just another institution but the *one* institution, that it is Christ's Body even though it bears the human marks of a social institution, then she will know the Church. She will not be loyal to the Church because of the minister or because of the people in the congregation to whom she is devoted. She will be loyal to the Church and the minister for whom she works because her attitude to the Church is in the right perspective: she is loyal to the Church because it is Christ's Body.

The church secretary should have a deep and sympathetic feeling for her employer. She should know that many times he is wrestling with the problems of his vocation and that he needs her support. There are many ways in which the concerned secretary can prepare herself for this understanding. She can attend conferences on the ministry of the Church, for example. She can read books on the professional ministry, some of which will be found listed as Suggested Readings in this book. She must seek to understand as best she can what her employer's vocation means to him, how he understands his relationship to his people and the community. Does he accept appointments on committees because he thinks that is expected of him, or does he really wish to contribute something to the issue with which the committee is concerned? Does he really know the community surrounding his church, or is his knowledge second-hand, the kind any one can acquire? If put to the test in a ticklish situation, would he have the fortitude to take a stand even if it meant severe criticism from his parishioners? What does it take for a man to dare to be different? What would it mean to him if the budget had to be pared or members were lost because of his stand on a controversial issue? How does he respond when he senses that his congregation is no longer with him?

INVOLVEMENT AND ITS DANGERS

When I lived on the Lower East Side of New York it was as the wife of one clergyman and the secretary of another. I think the secretaries in both church offices knew the clergy and people almost as well as they knew their own families. The church, the vicarage, the church office, the parish house—all were part of our lives and of the life of the church and the community. There was mutual involvement all along the line.

This kind of involvement has its rewards; it also has its pitfalls. It is extremely hard for a secretary, a pastor, or any other member of a church staff to be *truly* involved and yet remain objective. When one takes on, in a real, honest way, the heartaches, hopes, despairs, financial worries, and family problems of others, these become one's own to a great degree. Personal involvement lies heavily on the emotional life of the secretary, and it may be that some over-identification results—that is, the secretary so absorbs the emotional problems of the persons with whom she deals that their problems are added to her own. This sharing of burdens and experiences can be strengthening if the secretary is able to understand them as the burdens and experiences of others. If she is able to empathize with the people she deals with, able to feel their burdens without trying to carry the load herself, if she can lend her help and sympathy without overidentification, then she is likely to remain relatively objective and to the degree necessary for her own emotional health.

This does not apply only to the secretary. It applies also to the pastor. How many ministers find themselves bogged down in melancholy over the affairs of their parishioners? How many become excessively despondent over their inability to do more to help? How many men become so preoccupied with the deep conflicts of others that they themselves become noncommittal and tend to withdraw into a world of their own? The secretary, like the pastor, must frequently take a good, long look at herself, her abilities, and her *limitations,* and try to minister within the framework of her capabilities realistically assessed.

In her attempt to remain objective, the secretary should allow herself interests, recreation, and hobbies outside the sphere of her work. Actually, there are no activities that do not in some way bear at least indirectly on her life and job. To the committed Christian, all areas of life are ministry, even play. However, she is less likely to become overly involved in her relationships if she rounds out her work and balances her judgment by doing the kinds of things that refresh and stabilize. In this day and age there are endless possibilities. Hospitals and institutions appeal for volunteer help. Children's wards and homes need women who can provide entertainment and instruction. Political action groups and community organizations need many hands to become effective. The person who is occupied in trying to help others often forgets her own problems.

Out-and-out relaxation is important too. In small communities and large there are usually groups that offer fellowship and fun: choral groups, exercise groups, dramatic groups, bridge tournament clubs, interpretative dance groups, amateur painting classes, and the like. Almost all communities offer a variety of sports. The activity that appeals most to the secretary is the one she should choose, for she will be more effective in her work and bring a freshness to it when she herself has been re-created through such an acitivity.

PROTECTING THE MINISTER

The secretary should "learn" her employer and anticipate his needs. This is no different from what every secretary should do whether in the church or in business, and experience alone will help her here. She should study her boss, his way of doing things,

his sensitivities, his habits, *even his peculiarities.*
Nothing helps him more than the knowledge that his
secretary knows his needs in advance. He then can
forget most of the details and concentrate on the real
issues of his ministry.

This does not mean that the secretary should pry
into his private life. On the contrary, she should be
aware of the line between his public and private life,
and be very jealous of his privacy. She should find
ways always to protect him from parochial invasions
when he does not want to be bothered or disturbed.
Everyone knows there are calls that only the pastor
can handle, but everyone also knows that many of
the telephone calls and many people dropping in can
be handled by an able secretary or some other member of the staff. If a man is hard pressed to finish an
address or make preparations for an important conference, nothing is so welcome as a few hours alone,
free from interruption. The secretary should not give
the impression that she is protecting him from burdensome or difficult problems. But when the minister
is "off," he should rest content in the knowledge that
things are being well handled in his absence and that
his secretary will call him only for the most urgent
matters. He should be confident that she knows the
difference between trivia and something that should
be brought to his attention at once.

When I was an executive secretary in a large
urban parish with several thriving chapels, it was the

custom for any untoward events or requests to be channeled through me to the rector. Once I was wakened in the middle of the night by a young minister with the news that the church house in which he lived was on fire. I told him to call the fire department, which he assured me he had done already. I then asked him to join the firemen and find someone to keep telephoning me constantly, so I could decide whether or not to communicate the news to the rector. The fire was extinguished (the damage, fortunately, was slight), everyone finally got to bed, and the rector was notified in due time. This is, to be sure, a rather extreme example, but it does illustrate that some matters can be taken care of by someone other than the pastor, who already has his share of the burdens of the parish—and more.

If the right relationship exists between the secretary and the minister, an impression that she is trying to run the parish, or wants to do so, will never even arise. He and he alone is the head, and he alone is ultimately responsible. She must never forget this. At the same time he cannot be the head unless he has help. The secretary is his right arm, and he cannot function effectively without her. The minister himself must use discretion and prudence in deciding what he can and cannot tell his secretary. People talk to him because they know he will not betray their confidence. A secretary should never be offended when a usually loquacious clergyman "clams up."

There will be times when he feels he should not discuss certain matters, not because he believes his secretary will divulge the information, but because he feels they are purely pastoral in nature. The secretary should accept and understand such a decision as she accepts and understands his vocation. She should harbor no feeling of being excluded in such instances.

It behooves the secretary to find her place as the valued helper without trespassing on the minister's pastoral territory. When two persons work closely together for a long time, and the secretary has become very familiar with her work and position, it is easy fo her to assume duties and prerogatives that are outside her sphere of concern and responsibility. Without meaning to, she can find herself becoming *the* counselor, *the* confidante, *the* manager of the show. Particularly is this apt to happen when the pastor is absent from the parish a great deal and much is left to the secretary for attention. It is in such a situation that she will truly show her reliability and responsibility. She must not forget—nor let others forget—that she is acting only for the real head. She must in no way mar his image or undercut his authority.

I have known clergymen who allowed themselves to be emasculated by their secretaries. They had depended upon them to such a degree they found it difficult to make a private decision or move with certainty. It was not so much a matter of self-surrender as it was being "other-directed." They did not lose their identities entirely, but their personalities were dominated by the habits and views and expectations of their secretaries. The well-meaning secretary can become so oversolicitous of her employer and his task that she transfers *to* him her anxieties and un-certainties. Conflict then arises out of a conflict of roles. I do not mean to indicate that the secretary must not give true expression to her own individual-ity or that she must assume a false show of subservi-ency. I do mean that she should maintain her posi-tion and possess herself in such a fashion that the pastor's leadership is confirmed and strengthened.

GOVERNING BOARDS

The pastor treasures his secretary's good relation-ships not only with other members of the church staff and congregation, but also with the church's governing board, the members of which are chosen for their qualifications and because they are willing to give time and energy to the church. They are im-portant to the contentment and well-being of the minister. Their job is to be of help to him personally and to assist him in the many matters pertaining to the church outside the realm of worship and ser-vices, which in the main are his direct responsibility.

The secretary should attempt to know the members of the official board as well as possible, and their secretaries, too, if they have them. Hers should be a pleasant and friendly relationship, no matter what relationship exists between the individual member and the minister. Her manner should be respectful toward them, and she should be ready to assist them, regardless of the pressure of other matters. Well before meetings of the board or vestry, she should have prepared for the pastor the list of all items carried over from the previous meeting, announcements to be made, agendas, and exhibits. Any pertinent discussion at prior meetings that is liable for further discussion should be brought to his attention. After the meeting is over, the secretary's immediate responsibility is to begin to take care of those matters which were referred to the minister for handling—resolutions, correspondence, and so forth. Some items, because of their importance or because the minister alone has the information, will require his personal attention, but he should not have to be bothered with routine follow-up. This rule applies to the business of any and all other committees on which he serves or which he chairs.

Board members and vestrymen usually are good churchmen and interested in the welfare of the minister and his family, as well as the growth and management of the parish. It is because of this genuine interest and concern that the secretary will have to use care in distinguishing between concern and inquisitiveness. Without intending to do so, and certainly without malice, a secretary can inadvertently divulge information that easily could be misconstrued. Although this is true in her dealings with anyone, she should exert special care in the case of vestry or board members and members of the staff. The ease with which she can let something slip stems from her familiarity with these people, and an unfortunate sharing of confidences can result.

DUTIES OF AN EXECUTIVE SECRETARY

Fortunate is the pastor who, in addition to his assistant minister(s) and director of Christian education, has an adequate office staff: executive secretary, secretary, and church school secretary. In this case he is the head, and the executive secretary is his chief assistant. In most instances the director of religious education works on a more independent basis than other members of the church staff, because of the nature of her duties. She often reports directly to the pastor but often, too, through the executive secretary on general matters. With a multiple staff there will be problems of the division of labor and supervision that from time to time must be discussed. The executive secretary usually is responsible for selecting and training her own office help since she should know her field better than anyone else. But each person hired should be approved by the pastor and by the board or vestry if required by parish rules. The executive secretary should interview and screen all applicants, and then present the person's name and credentials to the pastor. Here, as in business, she must be cautious in making her recommendations. It is often tempting to employ a person with an engaging personality and appearance. These may be two very important requisites, but previous experience, technical skills, health, age, and education must also be carefully weighed.

I will not go into the methods of interviewing, screening, and selecting personnel. There are many good secretarial manuals which deal effectively with this phase of office procedure. By the time a secretary has reached the executive level, she should be experienced along these lines. I would add a word of warning, however, to the person being interviewed either by a minister or an executive secretary: she should obtain explicit information as to her vacation, her office hours, the amount of overtime expected, fringe benefits, and other items pertinent to the job. The explanation of these things is carefully emphasized in most business firms by the head of personnel, but I have known church secretaries who became unhappy and dissatisfied when the overtime proved more than they had anticipated or the vacation shorter than first mentioned. Office hours? "The usual." Fringe benefits? "Many." Vacation? "Some, I'll have to let you know." Insurance? "We're covered here." These are the kinds of answers a prospective applicant for a church position may hear, and they don't mean much. The person to be hired should know exactly what she can expect as well as what is expected of her.

Fortunate is the executive secretary who is able to train a cooperative group of loyal and dependable helpers. Bringing this to pass will depend in part on the individuals assembled, but to a large degree it will depend on her own ingenuity. She seldom will receive respect and loyalty unless she gives adequate time to training. A newcomer to an office should be patiently introduced to procedures and rules and then given additional duties after the initial training period is over. When one has been in a position for a long time, it is easy to become so accustomed to the routines that one forgets how difficult it can be for a new person to learn the ropes. A newcomer is baffled by nicknames and shortcuts, ecclesiastical terms, and church language. First impressions in an office are often hard to erase.

The secretary should share what information she can about the work and all that goes on in the church office. Nothing is more disheartening to subordinates than to be given the idea that they are being left out of things. It goes without saying that she will use discretion in this sharing, but she must make her staff feel that they really are part of the act. Although she may have seniority by many years and her ideas may be excellent, she should give all the staff full opportunity to share their views and to discuss office procedures. If the suggestions are not practical or the ideas feasible, the staff members should be told so and why. There is no better way to gain the backing of a working staff than to be straightforward. It will establish the executive secretary's honesty forthwith. Needless to say, her own prejudices should not be aired, but those of her staff, if voiced, should be heard and assessed.

The distribution of work and the assignment of duties is left to the executive secretary. Many employers prefer to deal exclusively through her, but some may prefer dictating to the person who does the transcribing. At any rate, it is through the executive secretary that such arrangements are handled.

The executive secretary's job is an exacting but satisfying one. Happy is she who can master it and at the same time gain the confidence and admiration of both her superiors and her subordinates.

TEAM MINISTRY AND CRISIS MINISTRY

I have spoken of the secretary in her position as an executive. There still is another important role that some secretaries are privileged to play. The team ap-

proach to the ministry is becoming popular within
some denominations, and there are indications that it
may become more widespread. In the team ministry
all members of the staff, including the secretary, are
on equal footing with the clergy. Acting together,
they form the nucleus of the group ministry and assume the necessary leadership in parochial affairs.
The secretary can make a contribution to such a
team, and every team ministry should include her.

The team ministry presents an interesting arrangement and can be very effective, but sometimes it
poses knotty interpersonal problems. Sooner or later
the question of authority arises. It can hardly be
avoided, and the secretary may find herself em-
broiled in conflict. She must use all her influence and
ingenuity to keep others from rocking the boat, so
to speak. A team ministry can also be demanding in
that the team members may have little or no privacy.
The constant companionship of others can become
wearing, and the subordination of one's will to the
decisions of the group can be frustrating. One dilemma the secretary may face in the team ministry is
the situation where she finds herself taking sides
against the pastor in a meeting. Needless to say, this
could have repercussions.

Because so much is happening today, a secretary
may well be employed in a parish that is frequently
in a state of crisis. Not all parish ministries are crisis
ministries, but perhaps they ought to be! At any rate,

many churches throughout the country are finding themselves face to face with crisis—especially the racial crisis. Are the church doors truly open to all men—or are they open as a token only? Housing, for example, is becoming the concern of neighborhoods and churches, and the differences of opinion that arise on this subject often result in setting neighbor against neighbor and church member against church member. The secretary should exhibit calm and patience whenever the minister's stand or the church's stand is under fire. The telephone will ring incessantly, and angry church or community members will want to talk with the pastor. When the secretary speaks with these people before they talk to the pastor, her own calm attitude can go a long way toward smoothing ruffled tempers.

When a situation of crisis exists in a neighborhood, the secretary can help keep her employer well informed. She should share with him what she hears in the community about current issues. If he asks her to, she should give him her assessment of the situation and what she thinks may be expected. Without belaboring the point, or perhaps even mentioning it, she should let him know that she is with him when he takes unpopular positions, that she, too, is aroused and excited when the Church is being the Church. At her post in the church office, in her life in the community, in her relationships with her friends and associates, she may find people speaking out forcibly and with candor. At such times her knowledge of the critical situation and her appraisal of it can be helpful to the minister seeking to lead his people amid the complexities of the modern age.

THE PASTOR'S WIFE

In a church office the relationship between the secretary and her employer's wife may be on a more friendly basis than were she employed elsewhere. Often the parsonage or rectory is near the church, but even when it is not, the minister's wife is frequently at the church taking part in various church activities. She may serve on several committees and thus find it necessary to call the church office frequently. When the minister is frequently away from the office on calls or in response to other commitments, her association with the secretary may become close. In such situations it is good for both parties when each is understanding of the other and each makes an honest effort to respect and assist the other. Too often, unfortunately, the giving is all on one side. Like some parishioners, the minister's wife may constantly ask favors of her husband's secretary. A certain amount of this is to be expected, and the secretary should attempt to include these requests in her schedule. When the relationship is as it should be, the secretary not only is willing but pleased to be of assistance.

However, I have known occasions when the wife acted as though the church secretary were her own secretary. Eventually, this false assumption is bound to cause resentment. Most church secretaries have plenty of work to keep them busy; many are even overworked. Constant demands from the minister's wife can become an appalling burden. Often the secretary hesitates to refuse and is embarrassed to speak of the matter to the minister. With dismay she simply adds the extra duties to her day's work. This lack of consideration will at length affect her attitude toward the pastor's wife and may also reflect itself in her attitude to him. She even may find herself shifting the blame to him.

How much grief would be saved if the wife were to make her requests for office help *through her husband*. When presented with a request from him, the secretary can easily make it known, for example, that she can complete the assignment only by letting the sermon go untyped. This procedure also enables the minister to estimate how often he can feel free to call upon his secretary to assume additional work. When he knows that she is pressed already, he can tell his wife so. The secretary will then be spared having to refuse the wife directly, which might antagonize her, or taking on the job while harboring ill will.

On the other hand, the secretary must conduct herself in such a manner that she does not become the "office wife." A possessive secretary can arouse jealousy, putting the minister as well as herself in a position open to criticism. She can even become a divisive element in the life of the parish. When the secretary knows her employer very well, when she knows his family and friends, when she shares his disappointments, his joys, his anxieties, her relationship to him is very personal. When she works closely with him, does many of his chores, arranges many of his day's activities, seeks to keep him happy and comfortable in the office, she is performing to some degree wifely duties. How can a person be personal and impersonal at the same time? The secretary does not need to be as cold and calculating as a piece of machinery; she does need to exert care lest she give any impression of intimacy. Good judgment and her woman's intuition ought to guide her. The secretary who has the love and respect of the minister *and* his wife is a happy and secure one.

GRIEVANCES

It is to be hoped that the relationship between the secretary and the minister will always be a good one and that they will work well together. However, there may come a time when misunderstandings arise. The secretary may feel that she has been criticized unfairly, she may feel that she has been overlooked on some occasion, or she may not agree with some of his decisions. The result is that for a time the job does not seem to go right. This is usually no more than a passing problem if the secretary feels free to talk frankly with her employer. One would hope she would do so. But sometimes the individual's personality and reticence preclude this, and she feels that she must discuss her position with someone else. To talk over personal grievances with other members of the staff, members of the vestry or board, or members of the congregation is often very unwise. Although they may be quite sympathetic and concerned at the time, the possibility always exists that conditions and loyalties will change; then the secretary's confidence may be violated or the pastor may receive a distorted report of the situation.

Discussing grievances, real or imagined, seeking guidance and advice, can clarify a situation at times. In the telling, new insights may be found; comfort and understanding from another may alleviate some anguish; and the advice of another may help solve a problem. The church secretary can find such help by going to an older and experienced minister. He will have had years of listening to woes and frustrations, and in his knowledge and from his experience he can offer wise counsel. Having been, or being now, the head of a church office, and knowing its ins and outs, he is in a special position to help her.

Then, too, almost every secretary has some older friend or acquaintance whose judgment she respects. (I say "older" because the years bring wisdom and tolerance.) Such a person would be pleased and perhaps flattered to be chosen as a confidant, and would be honest in evaluating the situation.

If the secretary is married, she can talk things over with her husband. He may tire of hearing the story repeated; at times he may appear annoyed with the whole thing; but he will be frank, sympathetic, objective—and maybe even a little amused! Sometimes what we need to see is that we are taking ourselves a little too seriously.

FRIENDSHIPS

The secretary in the church office may draw some of her friends from the congregation. Unless she shuts herself off completely from the mainstream of congregational activities, it is natural that she share some of her free time with those who have the same interests. Persons within an organization often are attracted to others who have mutual concerns and objectives, and they seek friendship and recreation with those with whom they work or mingle. The time the secretary spends outside her office hours is, of course, her own business. However, just as she would in any important position in any field, she guards herself and her office at all times. This does not mean she does not participate in healthy argument and dialogue with her friends, even if they are members of the congregation, but she does maintain a certain restraint. Church politics are not for her. Neither does she allow herself to be drawn into a discussion of the minister, members of the board or vestry, or other members of the staff. To do so is a poor policy in any office, but especially in the church office.

The church secretary must also be careful about socializing with members of the congregation when they visit the church office. Certainly it must be a place of hospitality, and all must be received with pleasure. I have mentioned some of the ways she can minister to those who come in. The prolonged social visit, however, can become a time-consuming habit, and she may have to remind a caller that she has to get on with her job. The pleasant but firm reminder, fortunately, works with most people.

DECORATING THE OFFICE

The trend toward simpler, more open styles in church architecture means that the church office, too, is in many places undergoing a change. The new look tends to be cheerful, airy, and imaginative.

Some ministers prefer to do their own decorating, but others, content to have their books and a few favorite pieces around, are happy to leave the office décor to the secretary and her helpers. It is a pleasant task to arrange offices that reflect good taste, an inviting atmosphere, and the minister's individuality. This applies not only to a new church building, but to old ones as well. For example, there are a number of art establishments that offer good, contemporary works of art at moderate prices. The secretary should keep abreast of good buys in tasteful religious art objects. Or, if there is absolutely no money for such purposes, she should try to borrow good pictures. We have no need today to rely on the sentimentally pious reproductions usually associated with church offices. The secretary should encourage any artists in the congregation to display their works. Many would be willing and happy to arrange an exhibit in the parish house.

PERSONAL APPEARANCE

No pastor wants his secretary to appear for work as though she were ready for a party, but neither does he want her to be drab and colorless. Dresses or suits in pleasant colors and of conservative style are always suitable in the church office. The secretary should attempt to acquire the art of dressing properly and using make-up attractively. Extreme styles in hair arrangement and make-up are, of course, bad taste. Eye make-up is suitable when used in moderation, and all cosmetics should be skillfully applied. The secretary who is attentive to her grooming and appearance is a compliment to her employer. It is a personal and thoughtful tribute to her position.

WORKING WITH THE NEW PASTOR

In some denominations the pastor remains in his parish as long as his services are acceptable to the majority of the congregation and as long as he feels that his ministry is effective there. In other denominations it is the practice to rotate ministers every several years, the length of time depending on the canons of that particular denomination. Often in small churches the pastor does not remain long since he is called to a larger place once he has gained experience.

In the first instance, the secretary and her employer have time to become a happy and cooperative team. In the latter instance, the church secretary will find herself trying to adjust to a new man very frequently. This in itself takes patience and understanding on both sides. In some cases it is the custom for the entire staff to resign when a new minister is called, in order to give him the privilege of hiring the kind of staff he prefers. Generally, such resignations are a courtesy only; usually the secretary and at least some others remain. Unless there is some specific reason, it is to the new pastor's advantage to keep the secretary, at least for awhile, since she can be of great assistance to him as he begins his new work. She, above all others, can afford to be quite frank about situations and problems involving the congregation, and it is expected that she will present to him her picture of the life of the congregation *without prejudice.*

On the other hand, the secretary must be ready to make adjustments in her own job and methods. The new pastor in all probability will have his own way of doing things and will expect her to adapt to his procedures. The spirit in which she makes this attempt will prove her loyalty to her new employer. She may receive constructive criticism and should accept it gracefully. Well-known routines provide comfort and confidence, but new and objective suggestions can prove to be stimulating and helpful. However close the secretary's friendship was to the former minister and his family, however great was her admiration for his ministry, however secure she may have been in her own relationship to the vestry or board, her obligation, when a new pastor arrives, is to *him.* This is not only a challenge; it is a duty.

Chapter 4
SOME SPECIFIC DUTIES

It is important that the minister spend ample time daily briefing his secretary and discussing with her various matters and scheduled activities. The secretary must know what is going on in order to do her work effectively and to act decisively. Many of the minister's conferences will be about the personal problems of his people, and so they will be strictly confidential. This does not mean that the minister does not share the responsibilities of the church office with his valued assistant, though in the case of confidential appointments, she need know only the general nature of the call so that she can greet the caller in a helpful manner.

RECEIVING VISITORS AND
MAKING APPOINTMENTS

The church secretary's contact with visitors brings all her qualities into play. As already stated, she will need, in addition to her sense of courtesy, tact, poise, good judgment, sympathy, and understanding. She has two duties with respect to office callers: first, her duty to her employer and his wishes, and second, her responsibility for the visitor and his requirements. A minister seldom tells his secretary how he expects her to respond to a particular caller, but it is helpful to tell her anything out of the ordinary that will enable her to make the visitor feel comfortable and expected.

Every person calling at the church office should be given a gracious greeting and prompt attention. Whether the greeting is formal or informal will depend on how well the secretary knows the caller. If the person calling seems under undue stress, the secretary may find it kinder to respect his privacy by casually continuing her work once she has made him welcome. If a person has to wait any length of time, she should explain why the minister is late and offer the visitor a book or magazine to read. When a visitor begins a conversation, the secretary should, of course, respond, but it goes without saying that she should make every effort to avoid controversial issues.

Some people seem to think that a minister should have time to see them at any hour of the day. It is often difficult for a person who has no appointment to understand that the pastor has responsibilities other than counseling. How many hours of a pastor's time could be saved and how much better his work could be organized, if members of the congregation recognized that the church office is a place of business, too. For some reason there are many who feel that an appointment or a limitation on their call is not necessary in a church office.

After she has worked with him awhile, the secretary will have a good idea which people the minister will see without appointment. If the caller states the nature of his visit, the secretary should decide whether to disturb the pastor or whether she should give the visitor another appointment. Unless the minister definitely is free and ready to receive callers, the caller should be assured that a future visit would be welcome, an appointment should be made then and there, so that the visitor has no feeling of being rejected. Of course, there will be callers who will not be put off, nor will they give any indication of the reason for their visit. Usually they say it is personal, but go no further. In a business firm the secretary can quite easily say that she makes all of her employer's appointments, personal and otherwise, and that she must know what the call is about. In the parish office, "personal" may mean something quite different. In these instances the secretary has no alternative but to interrupt her employer.

One difficult decision the secretary sometimes has to make is to determine whether a staff member should see the minister when he or she has no appointment. There is no question but that a pastor and his staff need to see each other frequently, but a staff member who continually drops by the pastor's office can consume endless time—time that may be needed at that particular moment for something more urgent. If the staff is large, the secretary can save her employer much wear and tear by setting up regular appointments for him with his staff members. This need not be a formality. When time is adequately scheduled, a staff member knows that the items he has for discussion will receive proper attention. The pastor will be more receptive and the staff member may well be better prepared for constructive conversation. This does not mean the pastor is inaccessible at other times; it does limit unscheduled meetings, however, for staff members then have the duty to think ahead about their needs.

It is the secretary's responsibility to see that appointments are changed if the occasion demands. She should handle all letters or telephone calls concerning appointments unless the minister himself wishes to write a specific letter or make a special call. She should remind the minister well in advance of each appointment, and should furnish him with any files or other pertinent information he may need for the appointment. Particularly is this true in the case of persons who habitually come for financial assistance. Almost all church offices have dependent and needy people who must receive what aid they can at the discretion of the minister. Seldom are there enough funds to meet such needs. It is a good policy to keep a file of each case, recording when a donation was made and the exact amount given. When requests are made of the pastor, the list will help him determine which cases are most urgent. The record is not aimed at making people "numbers" but at helping as many as possible. The secretary's files on problem families in the congregation and community are also helpful. These should be kept up-to-date with notations as to any illness in the family, the unemployment status of members able to work, school or drop-out records, and so forth. The secretary may learn many of these facts during her working day when the minister is involved in hospital visits, community activities, and the like. He will appreciate her ability to listen for him.

THE APPOINTMENT CALENDAR

It is imperative that the minister have a well kept, up-to-date calendar on which he can rely. The secretary will have to work out the system that is best for her and for her employer. No calendar is of much help if it is not checked daily, in fact many times daily. All church feast days, important and extra services, regularly scheduled services, regular committee meetings should be listed for the entire year. All previously scheduled activities from the previous year should be entered from the old calendar, and notes made about what is expected of the pastor on all occasions; for example, sermon, greeting, installation of officers, and the like. Making these notes at the time the calendar is being prepared saves frantic searching through files when the occasion is near at hand. All parish and community affairs should be listed whether or not the minister plans to attend. He may have a change of plans or wish to appoint someone to represent him. All appointments and family anniversaries should be posted so he does not make conflicting engagements.

His pocket calendar or date book should be brought up to date without fail each day. Special attention should be given to those entries he has made while absent from the office. The secretary should feel quite free to question her employer if an appointment he has made does not coincide with her calendar. He must then decide which appointment should be changed or postponed. I cannot overemphasize the care which must be given to calendars. The pastor *must* know at all times what his obligations are and what freedom he has for additional activities.

Since the minister's calendar is at the mercy of his secretary, there is one important thing she can do not only for his own welfare but for his family's as well. That is to keep one day a week clear, if possible, so that he can relax or spend some uninterrupted time with his wife and family. The clergyman may exist who systematically sets aside a day of rest and relaxation, but I venture to say that the majority scramble to find any free time. Like a doctor's, the pastor's profession is subject to unlimited hours and unscheduled emergencies. Yet to preserve his own health, both physical and emotional, he should have time away from the strain of his church duties.

A recent survey conducted among a group of ministers of one denomination showed that the average minister spent about twenty-five hours a week (exclusive of the time spent sleeping) with his family. The size of his church membership or the number of children still at home did not seem to make a difference. I would wager that the number of hours would not vary too much among the clergy of other denominations except in special cases such as sickness or age. Some people think that because they frequently see the pastor going into or out of his home that he spends most of his time there. Actually, because of his odd hours, scattered time, early services, and evenings out, his at-home time is usually much less than the parishioner guesses.

The secretary can perform a real service by blocking off free days well in advance. She may even do so in collaboration with his wife, so that social events and family outings can be more realistically arranged. Whatever the secretary can do to protect her employer from the hazards of occupational stress is a real contribution to his well-being.

CORRESPONDENCE

In a properly run business office, executives are happy to be relieved of all but the most pressing and important correspondence. Many ministers would have more time for pastoral matters if they would allow their secretaries to answer whatever correspondence they are capable of handling—and no girl or woman should be employed as a church secretary who is not to be trusted with the mail and allowed to use discretion as to what she should or should not take care of. Because many ministers have not had business experience, however, they simply do not know what to give to their secretary. (I am not speaking of strictly confidential correspondence. How it is handled depends on the circumstances of the occasion, though here, too, the pastor must learn to trust his secretary. Her morale will be good when she knows she is being depended upon to keep confidences and to be prudent. Her morale will be low when she gets the impression her employer does not think she is dependable.)

The secretary should read *all* of the mail that comes in (except as mentioned above). Only in this way can she keep abreast of what is going on. If the pastor seems reluctant to begin turning letters over to her to answer, she might attempt a breakthrough by reading the mail as she opens it and attaching a typed reply to any of the letters she can handle before taking the mail to his desk. He may find it a pleasant surprise to have part of the mail already out of the way. If he prefers to answer the letter in his own manner, he can still do so, of course. After a time the pastor will discover that his secretary can take care of a great deal of the mail over her own signature (he will need to read file copies for information only), and that she can also prepare much of it for his signature.

It does not take long for an alert secretary to learn to follow closely her employer's style of writing. I have known cases where it was virtually impossible to determine which one composed the letter, the styles being so similar. The technique is for the secretary to familiarize herself with her employer's style and tone. She should use his pet phrases, convey his personality, and write exactly as he would have dictated to her—only barring his grammatical errors, of course!

A correspondent expects his letter to be answered quickly, and well it should be. One way to expedite correspondence is for the secretary to reply over her own signature. In such cases the formality of the salutation will depend upon how well she knows the writer. Sometimes a writer is offended if his letter is answered by anyone other than the person to whom it is addressed. On the whole, however, if the writer is interested in information only, the secretary runs no risks in replying for her employer. This applies even to bishops and other dignitaries when the letters are routine. The knowledgeable church secretary will be able to tell which letters she can answer. She should guide herself by her knowledge of the facts, her experience in the office, and her familiarity with the situation or problem. (See *Appendix* A for sample correspondence.)

Everyone likes to have his name spelled and pronounced correctly. Just so, a person who holds an official or honorary position wishes to be addressed in the correct manner. Much of the correspondence in the church office will be directed to persons with titles, and it is imperative for the secretary to acquaint herself with the proper procedures for addressing such people. Many books are available which list the proper form of address for officials in all fields, and the secretary should have one at hand. (Here may I say that she should also be able to consult social, business, and government directories, a good quotation collection, reference books, and an atlas. Many government publications provide pertinent information and statistics, and they are available for nominal fees.)

SCREENING THE MAIL

Every secretary should work out a method for handling mail expeditiously. She should have a sim ple procedure for incoming and outgoing mail that is understandable to the minister—*and one that he is willing to use*. In most instances, the simpler the better. Even at the risk of being barked at, she should bring urgent mail to his attention again and again until it is cared for. Pastors do not deliberately neglect their correspondents; they do get bogged down in matters of the moment.

In a large corporation the setup is such that the head man can go away for an extended business trip or vacation. The staff is so large, and the work so well coordinated and distributed that only urgent matters need be thrust upon him while he is gone. In small offices, and in most church offices, the staff may not be large and, although the curate or assistants or supply minister may cover parochial matters, other work and mail continue. The way in which the secretary brings this to the absent pastor's attention depends in large part on his preference. I believe that as little as possible is best. All correspondence should be acknowledged. The secretary should dispose of everything she can by making a concrete answer, a referral, or, if the subject matter can wait, a simple acknowledgment. All accumulated mail should be kept in folders: these letters should be marked for his immediate attention, those for notation only; reports and general materials in which he might be interested should have a folder of their own. Magazines and other publications should be dated and stacked, with certain articles of interest marked for his perusal.

When the minister is away only the most urgent matters should be forwarded to him. It is well to keep a memorandum of the more important letters and other matters, however, so that the secretary can report readily to the pastor should he telephone.

In forwarding mail to someone who is traveling or on vacation, I have found it wise to number each envelope so that if any mail is lost it will be missed immediately and have a better chance of being traced.

FILES

Complete and accurate files are of utmost importance in any office. Many ministers leave the method of filing to their secretary. If a minister prefers a particular system, however, or is already accustomed to one, the secretary should adopt his preference. Whatever system is used, it should be one the pastor understands so that in the secretary's absence he can find a letter or a report himself. She should explain the system to him and show him its arrangement. Naturally, when he wishes folders or materials from the files, the secretary should be able to get them at once, but her files should be set up in such a fashion that he has no difficulty either.

In secretarial schools, students are taught various methods of filing. The two most important considerations are that the system used work well for the individual and that it be kept current. I know very well that filing is one of the things most secretaries leave undone when pressed for time. However, time found to keep the file box cleared will result in time saved in the long run. It is embarrassing not only for the employer but for the secretary if she spends unnecessary time looking for material or, worse still, is unable to find it at all. If the secretary has not had training in filing, she should study a good secretarial manual for information on the various systems, as well as on arrangement, indexing, labeling, and so forth.

The secretary generally has charge of filing the minister's personal correspondence. Among these papers will be confidential letters and reports. She is responsible for keeping these in private files accessible only to the minister and to herself. All personal and confidential material should be filed as promptly as it comes to her attention.

A "follow-up" file is of no use unless the secretary gives it constant attention. The correspondence that is pending, the matters that are due for discussion at meetings, the items to be referred to a committee, the reminder of an approaching address—all these are her responsibility. The "follow-up" file (in whatever form) is as necessary as the calendar, and items from it should be brought to the attention of her employer well in advance of the deadline, not at the last minute.

Most offices clear the files of correspondence and papers after several years. (The period usually depends upon the type of material and the statute of limitations.) In the church office, of course, all parochial files must be retained, although they can be classified and stored to preserve space. The destruction of any personal or confidential materials should be done only with the permission of or at the request of the pastor.

CHURCH RECORDS

Church records are as important as up-to-date files. Financial and parochial reports are necessary not only within the local church, but are required by most denominational headquarters. The individual church or parish will decide which is the most dependable system to use, but the system *must* be accurate. The membership or communicant list must be kept constantly up-to-date. In some denominations the number of active members governs the quota or the assessment by the national body. If the over-all membership list is incorrect, then the lists of various groups, organizations, Addressograph plates, will be out of kilter. All lists must be changed simultaneously in order to insure complete accuracy.

Membership cards should provide a complete history of every individual: date of birth, home and business addresses and telephone numbers, date of baptism, date of confirmation or reception, marital status, number and names and ages of members of the family, and other pertinent information. Some cards have space for the church activities in which each person is engaged. Transfers in and out of the parish, changes due to death or marriage, should be noted immediately. The card should afford a continuing history of the individual's relationship to his church.

When the parochial and financial records are kept correctly, the annual report to the congregation and to the denominational headquarters is easy to prepare. In addition, the records can be of considerable help in preparing reports such as comparative statistics, church attendance, age-group studies, and so forth.

The secretary who has the responsibility of recording the weekly pledges, making out financial reports, paying bills, and writing salary checks knows the effort that must be made to insure perfection. A church member has every right to be upset if his pledge has not been accurately recorded or if he receives mail at a former address long after he has changed his residence.

Church records are little histories. They tell stories of different generations. They provide legal evidence of birth. They serve sometimes as historical documents. They reflect a church's growth or decline. If properly kept, they provide insight and valuable information to a new pastor as he begins his ministry.

FILING SERMONS

One interesting phase of the church secretary's work is the typing, filing, and cataloguing of sermons. There are both simple and elaborate methods. The secretary should suggest the method she thinks would be effective and should try to discover her employer's preference. The sermons and addresses should be kept in durable notebooks or binders so that they can be removed easily. Each one should be dated carefully and kept in sequence, with notations made as to where and when it was delivered. If the minister is called upon frequently to address conferences or other gatherings, the secretary should have a more comprehensive set of files. She should have a cross index according to topics and texts. With this check it is not difficult to find a particular sermon in a hurry. It may well be that the pastor cannot remember the topic of a sermon he once delivered, but he may remember part of the text. As an example, if a sermon was entitled "The Church of God" and the text was "Go ye into all the world," the sermon would be indexed under *C*-Topics and also under *G*-Texts. Both indexes carry the dates and places of delivery. (Some useful examples of sermon filing may be found in *Appendix B.*)

EPILOGUE

In the foregoing pages we have discussed at some length the calling and work of the church secretary. I hope that what has been said there will, in some small way, help every church secretary who reads this book. I would like here, if I may, to bring into sharp focus the theme which is at the heart of all we have been discussing.

The church secretary's vocation, like others, is given her of God. Her abilities, her talents, her capacity for love, her wisdom—all are of God, and her task is to discover them and use them to His glory. She will do this both for her own soul's good and for the good of others.

Through worship, both corporate and private, the church secretary prepares and strengthens herself for her vocation, for her life within the church walls as well as for her life and the action without. Daniel Day Williams writes:

"Vocation is always a call to action. God, the creator, acts in his world, and seeks our redemption. God 'being in act' is reflected in man's bearing of his image. We are creatures for whom to live is to act. The meaning of 'action' is to be broadly taken here. It may be the internal act of sustaining courage in the face of fear, or that of concentration upon an intellectual problem. It may be the silent act of moral decision or strenuous participation in history-making forces. But it is through taking part in ongoing life, discovering what it is to succeed and to fail, to be right and to be wrong, and being baffled by the question of what is right or wrong that we come to possess our souls. Above all, it is in response to the call to action that we find our neighbor. We find him as friend, loved one, enemy, mystery, but we find him largely through what we do."

The church secretary's work is a consecrated service to the God whom she worships. Her job will lose its vital meaning unless it is made an offering to God of his freely bestowed gifts. It is the secretary's commitment to Christ Jesus which enables her to make this offering and to assume the responsibility to be, on her job, "the Church for others."

Her participation in the total life and ministry of the Church will depend in large measure on her ability to *see* the needs of all men and to give witness to the Gospel. There will always be the temptation to isolate herself in her office and to scorn the world and its problems. But the secretary's full commitment to Christ does not permit this. And when the temptation arises, the church secretary will do well to recall what Kyle Haselden has written:

"What happens when the gospel is retracted from all contact with the world is bad for the world, but it is also bad for the gospel. . . . The fault is not that the average churchman, lay and clerical, does not take history and the world seriously but that he does not take history and the world seriously in the light of the gospel, nor does he take the gospel seriously in the light of history and the world. The result is an abandoned world, a misdirected history, and an atrophied gospel. The more the gospel is withdrawn from the world—whether by the church, to cloister and protect the gospel, or by an autocratic world, to free itself from all moral tethers—the more seriously and swiftly does the gospel wither and lose its validity. . . . The churches were not called into being to rule the world but to serve it, not to reject the world but to embrace it with a redeeming love, not to withdraw from the world but to penetrate it with a healing and nurturing spirit."

I pray that no church secretary will ever be one of the indifferent.

Appendix A:
SAMPLE CORRESPONDENCE

The Reverend John Doe, S.T.D.
Church of the Redeemer
Fairfield, Virginia

Dear Dr. Doe:

Dr. Jones has received your kind invitation to address the Laymen's Club of the Church of the Redeemer on Wednesday, November 17, 1965.

He is happy that he is free on that date. He is looking forward to seeing you again and having the privilege of meeting your group of men.

The subject you suggest is satisfactory to him. He will send you a copy of his manuscript in sufficient time for publicity purposes.

> Sincerely yours,
>
> Katherine Smith
> Secretary to Dr. Jones

The Reverend James Smith
4820 Ferndale Avenue
New York 22, New York

Dear Mr. Smith:

Mr. Doe will be in New York City on Wednesday and Thursday, January 26 and 27. He would like to discuss with you the recent report of the Diocesan Committee on Housing.

Will it be convenient for Mr. Doe to call at your office on either of these days? He would appreciate your advising him as to the time and date if you are free to see him.

Sincerely yours,

Katherine Smith
Secretary to Mr. Doe

Mr. Robert Ames
412 Church Street
San Francisco, California

Dear Bob:

Mr. Doe left this morning for Seattle to attend the Conference on the Ministry to the Deaf. I will hold your letter for his attention upon his return later this week.

I cannot tell you how pleased he was with the report of your Building Committee. It appears that the goal is growing nearer each day.

Mr. Doe was asking me about your mother just before he left for Seattle. We hope her hospitalization will be brief. While Mr. Doe is out of town, she may expect our new assistant to visit her. His name is James Kirk.

When you return to the city, please call the church office. There are several points that I should have clarified before I have the Board minutes mimeographed.

Sincerely yours,

Katherine Smith
Executive Secretary to the Rector

The Right Reverend John Doe, D.D.
482 Minerva Street
New York 1, New York

Dear Bishop Doe:

We have received notification of your proposed visitation for Confirmation at the eleven o'clock service on December 12, 1965.

Mr. Jones has asked me to say that he and the members of the congregation are looking forward with pleasure to having you at St. Jude's on this occasion.

There will be a reception for you and for the confirmands immediately following the service.

Mr. Jones hopes that Mrs. Doe will be able to accompany you and that after the reception both of you will remain for luncheon at the rectory. Mrs. Doe will be hearing from Mrs. Jones in the near future.

Mr. Jones will be in touch with you early in December concerning details of the service.

Respectfully yours,

Katherine Smith
Secretary to the Rector

Mr. Roger Arnsworth
7124 North Swan Street
Burlington, North Carolina

Dear Mr. Arnsworth:

Dr. Doe is out of town for the next several days, but, in any case, he is not now the Chairman of the Committee on Race Relations.

Mr. Ernest Jones, the Church of the Saviour (Graham),

was appointed at the annual meeting last month. I am taking the liberty of forwarding your query to him for a reply.

Dr. Doe is returning on next Wednesday. If you so desire, I am sure he would be pleased to see you and to discuss informally the questions you have raised regarding the proposed resolution.

Please do not hesitate to call him after his return.

Sincerely yours,

Katherine Smith
Church Secretary

The Very Reverend John Doe, D.D.
Allsbrook Theological Seminary
2933 Meadowbrook
Geneva, New York

Dear Dean Doe (*or* My dear Dean):

Dr. Jones regrets very much that a previous engagement in Chicago, scheduled early in the year, will make it impossible for him to join the panel on *The Church in Action* on October 23, 1965.

It is an imposing list of speakers, and Dr. Jones has asked me to say that you are to be complimented in being able to bring together this distinguished group.

If the conversations are recorded and compiled, he would appreciate your putting his name on the list to receive a copy.

Sincerely yours,

Katherine Smith
Secretary to Dr. Doe

Appendix B:
SOME GENERAL HELPS

In her correspondence and typing the church secretary will use with great frequency religious and church terms, for which the rules of capitalization sometimes vary from denomination to denomination. That is to say, for example, in some denominations it is customary to capitalize all pronouns referring to God and Jesus, whereas in others these pronouns are not usually capitalized. The secretary, however, can always guide herself either by observing the convention followed in the denominations publications and magazines, or by the pastor's preference.

The titles of books of the Bible and of prayer books and hymnals, biblical names, and the names of denominations (even the shortened forms) are always capitalized.

The word *church* is often capitalized but not always. When this word means the church building, it is not capitalized. For example: (1) The Park Presbyterian Church is near my home. (2) There is a Presbyterian church near my home.

The title of a church official is capitalized when it refers to a specific person; for example, the Bishop of New Graham, the Moderator of the Synod. When titles are used generally, they need not be capitalized—A minister visits the hospital every afternoon.

When a person holds an academic degree, especially the doctorate, it is generally given as an abbreviation after his name. If there is doubt that an addressee possesses a certain degree, it is better to omit the degree than to attempt to supply it by guesswork. Then, too, the abbreviations for equivalent degrees vary—for example, a doctor of theology may be given Th.D. or S.T.D. A secretary can usually check her denominations clergy directory for the correct form of the addressee's degree.

The correct forms of address for officials of various denominations are usually listed in secretary's handbooks as well as in standard information handbooks. When the church secretary has any doubt in these matters, she should consult one of these sources. In some cases the local librarian can check the form for her.

Appendix C:
FILING SERMONS

BY DATE AND/OR CHURCH YEAR

Title	Vol.	Date	Church Year
The Church of God	IV-1	Jan. 3, 1965	Christmas II
Address to All Saints' Women's Group	IV-2 See: III-88	Jan. 7, 1965	Thurs. 1:00 P.M.
Renewal of the Church	IV-3	Jan. 10, 1965	Epiphany I
The Reality of Christ	IV-4 See: VI-3	Jan. 17, 1965	Epiphany II
What's in a Name	IV-5	Jan. 24, 1965	Epiphany III
The Remnant	IV-6	Jan. 31, 1965	Epiphany IV
Christianity and Crisis (Also used as Chap. 6 in *The Church and the World*	IV-7	Feb. 7, 1965	Epiphany V
The Christian and Power	IV-8	Feb. 14, 1965	Septuagesima
The Church in the New Society	IV-9	Feb. 21, 1965	Sexagesima
The Word (revised)	IV-10 See: II-19	Feb. 28, 1965	Quinquagesima
The Word and the Offering	IV-11	Mar. 3, 1965	Ash Wednesday
Our Victory in Christ	IV-12	Mar. 7, 1965	Lent I
Address—St. Mark's School, N.Y. Anniversary Dinner	IV-13	Mar. 8, 1965	Mon.-8:00 P.M.
The Mission of the Church	IV-14	Mar. 14, 1965	Lent II

Title	Vol.	Date	Chuch Year
Living on the Edge	IV-15	Mar. 21, 1965	Lent III
Invocation—Dedication of Central Methodist Church	IV-16	Mar. 25, 1965	Thurs.-3:00 P.M.
Greeting—Parish Annual Choir Service	IV-17	Mar. 26, 1965	Fri.-5:30 P.M.
The Saints of God	IV-18	Mar. 28, 1965	Lent IV
Our Present-Day Faith	IV-19	Apr. 4, 1965	Lent V
The Spirit-Filled Body of Christ	IV-20	Apr. 8, 1965	Whitsunday
Presentation—Children's Service	IV-21	Apr. 8, 1965	Sun.-3:00 P.M.
	See: III-2		

BY TOPIC

Topic: THE CHURCH'S ROLE IN THE CITY TODAY

Vol. VI-4 *C*

Cross Reference: Urban

1. Address at St. Jude's Church, Rochester, New York, at a meeting of inner-city clergymen, scheduled originally for 2/7/65, but canceled and rescheduled for 2/26/65.

   NO COPY but address based on article in *The Church Today* under the above title which appeared in the 11/10/64 issue.

   See also: Vol. III-1 *C*

2. Address at the Annual Laymen's Conference held at Christ Church, Burlington, Tuesday, March 9, 1965—dinner at 6:30—address at 8:00 P.M.

N.B.: 100 reprints of the article in *The Church Today* which appeared under this title in the 11/10/64 issue distributed at the conference.

3. Address at Michigan Diocesan Convention in Lansing, Monday, March 15, 1965, 2:00 P.M.

   N.B.: reprints of the article distributed.

4. Address at New York Clergy Conference at Holiday House held in New York City Thursday and Friday, April 10 and 11, 1965: theme of conference: the inner city and its problems.

   N.B.: Address revised.   Vol. IV-21 *C*
   Copies of Dr. Cole's *The City* distributed.

5. Address at Conference on Laymen's Work, Dallas, Texas, on Thursday, April 15, 1965, beginning at 10:00 A.M.

   N.B.: Revised address mimeographed and distributed. National series on the inner city made available. Printing of revised address made available by mail.

Topic: The Spirit-Filled Body of Christ   Vol. XI-2 *S*

1. Sermon at the Cathedral of St. Matthew, April 25, 1965, 11:00 A.M.

   TEXT: "When the day of Pentecost was fully come, they were all with one accord in one place."

   Acts 2:1

   Note: This is slightly revised version of sermon by the same title used on Whitsunday, Apr. 8, 1965. *See:* IV-20

2. Address at Epiphany Church, Graham, at Laymen's Luncheon on Wednesday, April 28, 1965, 12:30 P.M.

3. Sermon at Christ Presbyterian Church, Halifax, Sunday, May 9, 1965, 11:00 A.M.

4. Address during the city-wide Mission as follows:
    a) Hempstead, Long Island   5/17/65
    b) Brooklyn (Grace)   5/18/65
    c) St. Mark's, Bronx   5/19/65
    d) Calvary, Bronx   5/20/65

SUGGESTIONS FOR READING

DEVOTIONAL HELPS

Baillie, John, *Diary of Private Prayers*. New York: Scribner's Sons, 1949.

Ferris, Theodore, *Book of Prayer for Everyman*. New York: Seabury Press, 1962.

Heuss, John, *A Book of Prayers*. New York: Morehouse-Barlow, 1957.

Kelly, Thomas, *A Testament of Devotion*. New York: Harper & Row, 1941.

Little Book of Prayers. Mt. Vernon, N.Y.: Peter Pauper Press, 1960.

Smallzried, Kay, *Litanies for Living*. New York: Oxford University Press, 1964.

Wyon, Olive, *Prayer*. Philadelphia: Fortress Press.

GOSPEL, CHURCH, AND WORLD

Ayres, Francis O., *The Ministry of the Laity*. Philadelphia: Westminster Press, 1962.

Baly, Denis, *Besieged City: The Church in the World*. New York: Seabury Press, 1958.

Berger, Peter L., *The Noise of Solemn Assemblies*. New York: Doubleday, 1961.

Berton, Pierre, *The Comfortable Pew*. Toronto: Mc-Clelland & Stewart, 1965.

Boyd, Malcolm, *On the Battle Lines*. New York: Morehouse-Barlow, 1964.

Brunner, H. Emil, *Our Faith*. New York: Scribner's, 1936.

Campbell, Ernest Q., and Pettigrew, Thomas F., *Christians in Racial Crisis*. Washington, D.C.: Public Affairs Press, 1959.

Cellier, Frank Stephen, Ed., *Liturgy Is Mission*. New York: Seabury Press, 1964.

Congar, Yves, *Laity, Church, and World*. New York: Helicon Press, 1960.

Fosdick, Harry Emerson, *On Being a Real Person*. New York: Harper & Row, 1943.

Herberg, Will, *Protestant-Catholic-Jew*. New York: Doubleday, 1955.

Hofmann, Hans, Ed., *Making the Ministry Relevant*. New York: Scribner's, 1960.

Kelley, Alden D., *The People of God*. New York: Seabury Press, 1962.

Kraemer, Hendrik, *A Theology of the Laity*. Philadelphia: Westminster Press, 1958.

Micks, Marianne H., *Introduction to Theology*. New York: Seabury Press, 1964.

Packard, Vance, *The Status Seekers*. New York: McKay Company, 1959.

Phillips, J. B., *The Church Under the Cross*. New York: Macmillan Company, 1956.

Phillips, J. B., *Your God Is Too Small*. New York: Macmillan Company, 1960.

Pike, James A., and Johnson, Howard A., *Man in the Middle*. New York: Seabury Press, 1956.

Pike, James A., *A Time for Christian Candor*. New York: Harper & Row, 1964.

Robinson, John A. T., *Honest to God*. London: SCM Press, 1963.

Robinson, John A. T., *On Being the Church in the World*. London: SCM Press, 1960.

Stringfellow, William, *Free in Obedience*. New York: Seabury Press, 1964.

Trueblood, Elton, *The Common Ventures of Life*. New York: Harper & Row, 1949.

Wedel, Theodore O., *The Gospel in a Strange New World*. Philadelphia: Westminster Press, 1963.

Williams, Daniel D., *The Minister and the Care of Souls*. New York: Harper & Row, 1961.

Yates, Miles Lowell, *God in Us*. New York: Seabury Press, 1959; London: SPCK.

PRACTICAL HELPS

Becker, Esther R., *How to Be an Effective Executive Secretary*. New York: Harper & Row, 1962.

Hutchinson, Lois, *Standard Handbook for Secretaries*. New York: McGraw-Hill, 1964.

Lawrence, Nelda, ed., *Secretary's Business Review*. Englewood Cliffs, N.J.: Prentice-Hall, 1960.

Taintor, Sarah A., and Monro, Kate M., *The Secretary's Handbook*. New York: Macmillan Company, 1964.

Vernes, Jean, *The Secretary's Guide to Dealing with People*. New York: Parker Publishing Co., 1964.

SPECIAL PROBLEMS

Bowers, Margaretta K., *Conflicts of the Clergy*. Camden, N.J.: Thomas Nelson & Sons, 1963.

Cantoni, Louis and Lucile, *Counseling Your Friends.* New York: William Frederick Press, 1961.

Dicks, Russell L., and Kepler, Thomas S., *And Peace at the Last.* Philadelphia: Westminster Press, 1953.

Northridge, W. L., *Disorders of the Emotional and Spiritual Life.* New York: Channel Press, 1961.

Oates, Wayne E., *Anxiety in Christian Experience.* Philadelphia: Westminster Press, 1955.

Oates, Wayne A., Ed., *The Minister's Own Mental Health.* New York: Channel Press, 1961.

Rogers, William F., *Ye Shall Be Comforted.* Philadelphia: Westminster Press, 1950.

Westberg, Granger E., *Good Grief.* Philadelphia: Fortress Press, 1962.